GOING GOING GONE

100 ANIMALS AND PLANTS ON THE VERGE OF EXTINCTION

BLOOMSBURY

LONDON · NEW DELHI · NEW YORK · SYDNEY

Published 2013 by Bloomsbury Publishing Plc,
50 Bedford Square,
London WC1B 3DP

Copyright © 2013 by Think Publishing Ltd
A Think Book

Copyright © 2013 photographs as listed on page 222.

The right of Think Publishing Ltd to be identified as
the author of this work has been asserted by them in
accordance with the Copyright, Designs and Patents
Act 1988.

ISBN (print) 978-1408-1-8630-5
ISBN (ePub) 978-1408-1-8632-9

A CIP catalogue record for this book is available from
the British Library.
This book is produced using paper that is made
from wood grown in managed sustainable forests.
It is natural, renewable and recyclable. The logging
and manufacturing processes conform to the
environmental regulations of the country of origin.

Printed in China by C&C

10 9 8 7 6 5 4 3 2 1

Going Going Gone is dedicated to the
wildlife of the world, and to the many people
who work hard to protect it.

CONTENTS

CONTENTS

CONTENTS

FOREWORD

Humans share this planet with eight to 10 million other species, most of which have yet to be described. We have documented about two million species and of those we have assessed the conservation status, or extinction risk, of fewer than 70,000.

However, these assessments provide important insights into the status of the world's species. We now know that roughly 20% of all vertebrates (mammals, birds, reptiles, amphibians and fish) are threatened with extinction and initial assessments of plants and invertebrates indicate that 20% of all life forms are likely threatened. We also know that almost all these declines have been driven by human activity such as habitat loss, species introductions, exploitation or climate change – most of which are reversible. But with one-fifth of the world's species threatened with extinction, where do we start?

In this book you are introduced to a broad range of species that are threatened with extinction and the dedicated conservation organisations that are fighting to protect them. The future of these species is extremely important as their destiny is likely entwined with the 20,000 or more other animals, plants and fungi known to be threatened. If we cannot save the 100 species presented in this book, many of which are iconic, then what hope is there for other threatened creatures, most of which are currently receiving little or no conservation attention?

The future of the 100 species here is essentially a test of our values or attitudes towards other forms of life. If we are able to commit to these species and ensure their protection, we are well on our way to a future where all species on the planet are valued.

Professor Jonathan Baillie
Director of Conservation Programmes
Zoological Society of London

INTRODUCTION

Almost daily our global media – television, newspapers, the internet and blogosphere – tells us that one more of our planet's precious species has come to the brink of extinction, that a formerly pristine habitat is disappearing, that the entire planet is losing its biodiversity.

And it really does seem to be largely our fault. We're using the Earth's resources unsustainably; our expanding cities are consuming ever more land, leaving less for the wildlife; our throwaway lifestyles are polluting both land and oceans; our actions are leading to unnaturally fast climate change. There are so many problems, so many mistakes, so much to put right, that it seems impossible to know the right thing to do, to stem the tide of destruction and prevent the constant loss.

But, fortunately, there are people who are trying to find the answers. All around the world, charities, agencies and other organisations are working round the clock to change the picture going forward. Between them, their staff, their members and their volunteers, they're working to protect delicate habitats and the wildlife that needs them, and alter our perceptions of the natural world so that we live our lives more effectively and sympathetically to our environment. Their task is huge, and frequently thankless – and that's why this book has been compiled.

We wanted to show the range of threatened species, from the iconic to the unknown. We wanted to show the work that was being done across the world by organisations both large and small to preserve these plants, animals and environments and to show how we, as individuals, could contribute to this effort.

So we asked 100 conservation, scientific and research organisations from around the world to pick just one species, subspecies, animal group or habitat that needs saving – one symbol of the work that they do and the problems that they face, to write about it and to demonstrate how other individuals can help them with their efforts.

The range of contributors has been genuinely global. We have heard from such international groups as BirdLife International and the Worldwide Fund for

INTRODUCTION

Nature, as well as from tiny regional teams such as Painted Dog Conservation and The Scaly-sided Merganser Project.

We heard from conservationists throughout the world in all continents, from Europe to Australasia, from Africa to Asia and the Americas. The mix of wildlife highlighted has been equally as broad. While well-known icons of conservation, such as gorillas, tigers, elephants and rhinoceroses, were naturally nominated for the book, there are also vignettes of many far less well-known, but equally struggling species, such as the Argali Sheep, the Blue-grey Taildropper (a colourful slug), the Humphead Wrasse (a rather charismatic fish) and the Tomistoma (a species of crocodile with a particularly slender snout). Among the 100 included are plants and animals found only in a tiny restricted area and some so rare that there are less than 100 individuals still known to exist in the wild.

As you read through the book, you will probably find your personal favourites among the species. You'll be moved by their plight, and by the efforts of the organisations that are trying to help them. If you're moved to do something to help one or two of them as well, then all the better.

The wildlife and habitats in this book are disappearing much too fast. Unless we do something now, they will be gone for ever.

STATUS REPORT

I n most cases, the species chosen are on the IUCN Red List, a global list of more than 16,000 creatures that have been evaluated by The World Conservation Union, the world's largest conservation network. Where relevant, the status of the species is shown on its pages by one of the following criteria:

EXTINCT IN THE WILD: Known only to survive in cultivation, in captivity or as a naturalised population (or populations) well outside the past range.

CRITICALLY ENDANGERED: Considered to be facing an extremely high risk of extinction in the wild.

ENDANGERED: Considered to be facing a very high risk of extinction in the wild.

VULNERABLE: Considered to be facing a high risk of extinction in the wild.

NEAR THREATENED: Close to qualifying for, or is likely to qualify for, one of the above categories in the near future.

LEAST CONCERN: Widespread and abundant wildlife are included in this category, although they may be regionally threatened.

For more information, please visit www.iucn.org.

For some entries, CITES references are given. CITES is the Convention on International Trade in Endangered Species, and many thousands of species are protected by CITES against overexploitation through international trade. All assessed species fall into one of three Appendices:

APPENDIX I: Threatened with extinction.

APPENDIX II: Not necessarily threatened with extinction, but may become so unless trade in specimens is subject to strict regulation.

APPENDIX III: Not necessarily threatened with extinction globally, but assistance has been requested at national level in controlling trade.

Many countries also run their own national categories of conservation importance, which are referred to in some of the entries.

AFRICAN ELEPHANT

'IT IS ESTIMATED THAT BETWEEN 25,000 AND 50,000 ELEPHANTS WERE KILLED FOR THEIR IVORY IN 2011. THE LAST TWO YEARS (2011–2012) HAVE BEEN AMONG THE MOST DEADLY EVER FOR ELEPHANTS'
IFAW

Elephants intrigue and fascinate us – we marvel at their size, their complex way of communicating and their ability to 'never forget'.

Yet time is running out for the world's largest land mammal. During the 1980s, Africa lost half of its 1.3 million elephants before a global ban on ivory trade was introduced to stop the relentless slaughter.

Elephants are a keystone species and killing them for their ivory has an effect on the entire ecosystem. Poaching causes emotional and social distress to entire family groups and elephant society at large as they are highly intelligent, sensitive animals that are known to mourn their dead.

In early 2012, IFAW raised the alarm as hundreds of elephants were slaughtered in Cameroon. Sadly, inadequate protection for elephants on the ground is still continuing to drive poaching and the illegal ivory trade.

Most illegal ivory is destined for Asia, and China in particular, where it has soared in value as it is being snapped up by wealthy investors and coveted as 'white gold'. The situation has worsened recently as legal ivory, which China bought from the stockpile sale from southern Africa in 2008, has boosted demand, encouraging illegal ivory trade and the poaching of elephants to meet market demand.

To stop the killing, every day, across the globe, IFAW works with enforcement agencies and local communities to ease situations of human-elephant conflict; to build enforcement capacity within parks and reserves; and to educate the public on the current threats to elephants.

COMMON NAME: African Elephant

SCIENTIFIC NAME: *Loxodonta africana* (the African Forest Elephant – *Loxodonta africana cyclotis* – is widely regarded as a subspecies)

SIZE: Up to 4m at the shoulder.

STATUS: Vulnerable.

POPULATION: It is likely that the total continental population estimate is in the range of 420,000 to 650,000 African elephants with just three countries, Botswana, Tanzania and Zimbabwe accounting for well over half of these elephants.

LIFESPAN: In the wild, African Elephants live for around 60 years.

RANGE: Sub-Saharan Africa, inhabiting areas of forest, savanna, grassland and desert.

THREATS: The ivory trade, hunting, bushmeat, habitat loss and human-elephant conflict threaten to drive the species to the brink of extinction.

WHAT YOU CAN DO...

- Visit www.ifaw.org to find out more about our work protecting elephants from poaching and the illegal ivory trade across the globe.

- Avoid buying anything that is made from wild animals, such as elephants, including ivory jewellery or trinkets, elephant leather wallets or elephant hair bracelets.

AFRICAN PENGUIN

'MAJOR THREATS TO AFRICAN PENGUINS ARE THE LACK OF READILY
AVAILABLE PREY NEARBY, AND POLLUTION OF THEIR HABITAT BY OIL SPILLS'
UNIVERSITY OF BRISTOL

The endangered African Penguin used to be known as the Jackass Penguin for its donkey-like bray. Growing to around 55cm tall, each bird boasts a unique pattern of black spots on its chest.

At the turn of the last century, around three to four million African Penguins were thought to have thrived around the coasts of South Africa and Namibia. In 2000, the population was estimated to be around 200,000. Today the population has fallen much further to around 50,000.

African Penguins return to the same nesting colonies year after year – such as on South Africa's Robben Island. Once famous for its prison, which held former President Nelson Mandela, the island is now a UNESCO World Heritage Site and holds around 10% of the world's African penguin population.

Major threats to these birds are the lack of readily available prey nearby, and pollution of their habitat by oil spills. Lying in the middle of major shipping lanes, Robben Island has seen several incidents, with the worst to date occurring in 2000 when 13,000 penguins were oiled.

Researchers from the Universities of Bristol and Cape Town are collecting data that will form the basis for any long-term closures of fisheries around penguin colonies in South Africa – a measure that could aid the conservation of the blighted bird. The team also collect any oiled birds they find and send them to the local rehabilitation centre (SANCCOB), and have designed an automatic recognition system that may eventually allow remote monitoring of up to 90% of the penguins.

COMMON NAME: African Penguin

SCIENTIFIC NAME: *Spheniscus demersus*

SIZE: Normal standing height 55cm.

STATUS: Endangered.

POPULATION: Around 50,000 individuals in total, and decreasing.

LIFESPAN: Around 16 years in the wild.

RANGE: Twenty-five islands and four mainland sites in Namibia and South Africa.

THREATS: Main threats include competition with fisheries, hunting and petrochemicals.

University of BRISTOL WHAT YOU CAN DO...

- Support research by the Universities of Bristol and Cape Town by joining an Earthwatch expedition to Robben Island, to help conserve this species and their fragile habitat.

- Find out more about penguin projects at the Bristol Conservation & Science Foundation or the Bristol Zoo Gardens.

AMAZONIAN MANATEE

'THE AMAZONIAN MANATEE ONLY PRODUCES ONE CALF EVERY THREE YEARS MAKING THEM HIGHLY VULNERABLE. HOWEVER, CONSERVATION EFFORTS IN SOME AREAS SHOW THAT LOCAL HUNTERS CAN BECOME MANATEE GUARDIANS'
NATÜTAMA

All over the Amazon region, fishermen say: 'You have to be really lucky to see a manatee.' It isn't just because their snouts are so difficult to spot in the murky river waters and lakes – it is because Amazonian Manatees have been hunted for their meat and hides since pre-Columbian times and can no longer be found in many parts of their previous range.

Flood time in the Amazon provides manatees with rich banquets of floating vegetation, but low water often involves months of fasting; climate change has brought droughts that strand manatees in pools where they may die, or else make easy prey. Migrating between the lakes and rivers is an annual risk, especially now that fishermen stretch nets across channels, with manatee calves often becoming entangled. The calves are engaging and are sold illegally as pets, though few live long outside their natural environment.

Amazonian Manatees are secretive with good reason; despite their size they leave no ripples when breathing and their great paddle-shaped tails rarely break the water surface. Although their aquatic habitat is being reduced by dams, pollution and boat traffic, there are still manatee populations in parts of the Amazon that could survive if there was effective enforcement against illegal hunting. In one area where local communities actively monitor and protect the species, people say they are seeing more manatees.

COMMON NAME: Amazonian Manatee, Vaca Marina (Spanish), Peixe-boi (Portuguese)

SCIENTIFIC NAME: *Trichechus inunguis*

SIZE: Up to 2.8m length.

STATUS: Listed as vulnerable by the IUCN and varies from endangered to critically endangered in the countries where the species occurs.

POPULATION: There are no figures for overall population.

LIFESPAN: Amazonian Manatees are thought to start breeding at five to seven years old and can live more than 40 years.

RANGE: The River Amazon and the main tributaries and lake systems that lie below rapids and waterfalls in the Amazon basin. There are manatees in Brazil, Colombia, Ecuador and Peru.

THREATS: The main threat is hunting for food, despite the fact that manatees are protected by law throughout their range. More recently, incidental catch in fishing nets, climate change and habitat loss have contributed to the decline of manatees in many areas.

WHAT YOU CAN DO...

- Help to preserve the ecosystems and cultures of the Amazon Basin by learning about them and raising awareness so that endangered species are given better protection in accordance with local community values.

- Support the Natütama Foundation's conservation and education work with donations that contribute to the subsistence of Ticuna indigenous educators and fishermen (contact: fundacionnatutama@yahoo.com, web page: www.natutama.org). Visit our Environmental Interpretation Centre in the Colombian Amazon.

AMUR LEOPARD

'THERE ARE THOUGHT TO BE FEWER THAN 50 AMUR
LEOPARDS LEFT IN THE WILD'
AMUR LEOPARD AND TIGER ALLIANCE

The Amur Leopard, also known as the Far Eastern Leopard, is the northernmost of all leopard subspecies, found in the Russian Far East and Northern China, where it shares its habitat with Amur tigers. Sadly, these beautiful big cats, well adapted for snowy winters with their long, thick fur and pale colouring, are threatened by poachers and habitat loss. There is now just one single population of Amur Leopards left in the wild, numbering fewer than 50 individuals. To combat the threats facing them, the Zoological Society of London (ZSL) and its partners in the Amur Leopard and Tiger Alliance (ALTA) implement conservation programmes in Russia aimed at protecting these magnificent yet vulnerable big cats. ALTA supports anti-poaching teams, fire-fighting brigades, Amur Leopard population counts, wildlife health monitoring, and education and outreach projects. They also support a compensation scheme to farmers who lose livestock to leopard depredation, thus preventing retaliation killings.

ZSL and Moscow Zoo coordinate the European/Russian zoo breeding programme and the global zoo breeding programme for the Amur Leopard. Conservationists aim to reintroduce leopards from these breeding programmes into the wild, establishing a second population within the Amur Leopard's historical range. Although the remaining wild population does appear to be slowly increasing, the Amur Leopard is still at very real risk of becoming extinct.

COMMON NAME: Amur Leopard

SCIENTIFIC NAME: *Panthera pardus orientalis*

SIZE: Up to 140cm in length with a tail length of up to 90cm. Shoulder height up to 80cm.

STATUS: Critically Endangered.

POPULATION: Fewer than 50 individuals are thought to remain in the wild, but frequent counts using camera traps and snow tracks indicate the population is stable.

LIFESPAN: Probably up to 15 years in the wild and few years longer in zoos.

RANGE: South-west Primorski Krai; a small patch of land in the Russian Far East near Vladivostok and the North Korean and Chinese borders.

THREATS: Poaching of leopards and their prey species; habitat loss due to frequent forest fires and economic development projects.

WHAT YOU CAN DO...

- Sign up for ALTA's newsletter and discover what they are doing by visiting www.ALTAconservation.org.

- The Amur Leopard is 10 times more endangered than the Amur Tiger and needs more friends, so spread the word by following ALTA on Facebook and Twitter (@AmurALTA) and help raise much-needed funds. 100% of donations go straight to the field.

ANCIENT WOODLAND

'ANCIENT WOODLAND IS ONE OF THE GREAT GLORIES
OF THE UK'S NATURAL HERITAGE'
THE WOODLAND TRUST

Imagine the outrage if a nationally important historic building was threatened by demolition. Yet nature's equivalent, our ancient woods, are threatened by destruction due to the pressures of development and modern life.

Ancient woods provide our richest wildlife habitat, and are home to more threatened species than any other UK habitat. These national biodiversity treasures are places of inordinate beauty, providing living archives with rich historical and cultural associations. Ancient woodland is finite, so what remains is precious and irreplaceable. Remaining ancient woodland is scarce and fragmented, covering around 2% of the UK, but the vast majority of ancient woodland has no national designation. In fact, ancient or otherwise, the UK is one of the least wooded places in Europe. Only 12% of the UK's landscape is wooded compared with an average of 44% in other European countries.

Tree pests and diseases that are new to the UK have increased dramatically in recent years. While disease and decay are a natural part of ecosystems, this unprecedented increase has been accelerated by human activity. Coupled with climate change and land use pressures, this poses a severe threat to the survival, health and ecological functioning of trees and ancient woodland, and the species they support.

COMMON NAME: Ancient woodland – UK native species like pedunculate or sessile oak, beech, hornbeam, hazel, field maple, ash, wild service, hawthorn, blackthorn, spindle and wild cherry

AREA: Around 351,100ha of ancient woodland survive in England; 62,100ha in Wales, 148,200ha in Scotland and 999ha in Northern Ireland. Remaining fragments cover only 2% of the UK.

LIFESPAN: Ancient woodland is land which has been wooded continuously for at least 400 years, often much longer. Some ancient woods go back to the last ice age, which ended about 11,000 years ago.

RANGE: Ancient woods and trees are thinly scattered across the UK landscape in urban and rural areas.

THREATS: Tree pests and disease, development of land for industry, housing, roads and airport expansion, and commercial forestry.

WOODLAND TRUST

WHAT YOU CAN DO...

- Support the work of the Woodland Trust, the UK's leading woodland conservation charity; for more information, visit www.woodlandtrust.org.uk.

- The Woodland Trust strives to tackle tree disease in the most effective way to protect ancient woodland. To find out more, visit www.treedisease.co.uk.

ANDEAN CONDOR

'THIS ICONIC BIRD IS NOW ALMOST ABSENT
FROM THE NORTHERN PARTS OF ITS RANGE'
WILDLIFE CONSERVATION SOCIETY

A classic flagship species, the Andean Condor is the magnificent symbol of the high Andes. The condor is also an especially significant cultural reference and is revered by many of the Andean indigenous peoples. Sweeping majestically across high Andean landscapes on a 10ft wingspan, individuals have huge home ranges and political boundaries hold no meaning for the enormous condor.

Unfortunately, the Andean Condor is in trouble. It has almost disappeared from the northern portions of its range in Colombia, Ecuador and Venezuela. Habitat alteration and disturbance are important threats for the Andean Condor, but they are particularly vulnerable because of their size, their conspicuous scavenging behaviour and the relative ease with which birds can be targeted. Although the bird is traditionally revered, some Andean communities blame condors for a portion of their livestock losses. Studies on population size, ranging behaviour and conservation status are needed to help design appropriate conservation strategies.

COMMON NAME: Andean Condor

SCIENTIFIC NAME: *Vultur gryphus*

SIZE: Up to 135cm in height with a wingspan of up to 3m.

STATUS: Near-threatened

POPULATION: Approximately 6,200 individuals.

LIFESPAN: Approximately 50 years.

RANGE: Colombia to Argentina and Chile along the Andes.

THREATS: Habitat alteration, direct persecution through hunting, nest disturbance and carcass poisoning from aggrieved livestock owners due to perceived and probable livestock predation, and capture, use and eventual death or injury in Andean festivals in Peru.

WHAT YOU CAN DO...

- You can contribute to the conservation of the Andean Condor by visiting and supporting the high Andean protected areas of Bolivia, such as Apolobamba, Cotapata and Eduardo Avaroa. Log on to www.sernap.gob.bo. This will further enforce the concept that wilderness and wildlife can help pay for itself through ecotourism.

- You can also help save wildlife and wildlands by making a donation to the Wildlife Conservation Society, www.wcs.org.

ARGALI SHEEP

'IN MONGOLIA, WIDESPREAD POACHING HAS CONTRIBUTED TO THE SPECIES' DECLINE'
EARTHWATCH

It is the largest sheep in the world – some males have been known to weigh in at over 200kg – the Argali roams wild among mountains, steppe valleys and rocky outcrops, ranging from central Uzbekistan to China.

In Mongolia, widespread poaching has contributed to the species' decline in the region, while the distinctive corkscrew horns sported by the rams are used in traditional Chinese medicine. Argalis also face strong competition for food from livestock, brought in by local, nomadic farmers who sometimes own dogs that chase and kill the Argali. There is currently insufficient law enforcement in place to protect this unique ungulate.

An Earthwatch initiative is investigating Argali Sheep ecology in the Ikh Nart Nature Reserve of the Mongolian Steppe to help develop a long-term conservation management plan for the species and its habitat. Through fieldwork, and by working with local herders, the project has already seen great success. Since it began, the population of Argali in Ikh Nart has doubled and dispersal from Ikh Nart has led to the establishment of surrounding populations as well. In 2009, the United Nations Development Programme selected Ikh Nart as one of two model protected areas, and in 2012 the project scientists were invited to develop management guidelines for mountain ungulates in Central Asia.

Most importantly, the work has stimulated active management by the local area's authorities, including the creation of a protected areas office, ecotourism development to help pay for the costs of managing the park, and an active education programme.

COMMON NAME: Argali Sheep

SCIENTIFIC NAME: *Ovis ammon*

SIZE: Up to 135cm at the shoulder.

STATUS: Near-threatened worldwide. Endangered in Mongolia.

POPULATION: Most recent population estimate in Mongolia is about 12,000 animals (2011).

LIFESPAN: About 10-13 years.

RANGE: The Argali occurs over a vast geographical range, from central Uzbekistan to China, including Afghanistan, Nepal and Pakistan.

THREATS: Over-hunting and poaching; competition; displacement and possibly disease transmission by domestic livestock; and habitat loss.

WHAT YOU CAN DO...

- Join Earthwatch project *Wildlife of the Mongolian Steppe*, and help conserve this stunning wilderness, and all the species that call it home.

- Donate to Earthwatch to help our scientists continue their world-class environmental research, to promote the understanding and action necessary for a sustainable environment.

ASH

'WITH ASH DIEBACK, WE ARE FACING TREE DEATH ON AN UNPRECEDENTED SCALE'
THE TREE COUNCIL

Ash, the third most common tree in Britain, is a native deciduous broadleaf that occurs in more 1km squares of the country than any other big tree. Large spreading Ash trees can often be seen in hedgerows, where they host up to 68 species of invertebrates and over 500 species of lichen. With high wildlife value, they are nesting sites for redstarts, woodpeckers and nuthatches. They can also thrive near smoke and pollution, so are good urban dwellers, and provide timber where strength and flexibility are needed.

Ash dieback is a fungus that is killing our native Ash trees. Spread via spores from fruit bodies on leaf litter, once airborne they may carry for distances of 30km. Infection quickly causes leaves to wither as the disease enters the tree system. In young trees, loss can occur within two growing seasons, though some older trees have survived for much longer. However, it seems likely that these will also eventually succumb.

We are facing tree death on a scale not seen since the ravages of Dutch Elm disease, when The Tree Council was launched to champion repopulation of trees in the landscape. The priority now is to monitor, manage and slow the inevitable decline where possible, while field research is carried out to try to find a resistant strain to recolonise woodlands, hedgerows, countryside and towns. Tree Wardens, skilled community-based volunteers, are key to this process as they monitor spread and search for unaffected specimens.

COMMON NAME: Ash

SCIENTIFIC NAME: *Fraxinus excelsior*

SIZE: Up to 30m.

STATUS: Threatened and Vulnerable.

POPULATION: In Britain in 2012, estimated at around 125.9 million mature Ash trees plus 1.6 billion young trees.

LIFESPAN: Under average climate and soil conditions, the Common Ash may make 200 years, though there are some ancients thought to be 300-350 years old.

RANGE: Spread across the UK more widely than any tree except Hawthorn. European distribution from coastal Norway to the Mediterranean shoreline.

THREATS: *Chalara fraxinea*, an airborne fungal disease commonly known as Ash dieback, which can result in crown dieback, splitting and cracking of the stem and eventual death of the tree. It is endemic across mainland Europe and is now present in UK trees.

THE TREE COUNCIL

WHAT YOU CAN DO...

- Become a Friend of The Tree Council (www.treecouncil.org.uk/friends) and support our ash education, campaigning and fieldwork, or become one of our volunteer Tree Wardens and take practical action in your community.

- Learn the signs of ash dieback at www.forestry.gov.uk/chalara; notify the Forestry Commission of suspected outbreaks at www.forestry.gov.uk/treealert. Download the annotated pictorial guide at www.treecouncil.org.uk.

ASIAN ELEPHANT

'ELEPHANTS CREATE WATERHOLES THAT HELP OTHER ANIMALS IN THE DRY
SEASON AND THEY HELP THE FOREST REGENERATE BY SPREADING FRUITS
AND SEEDS – THEY HELP TO PROTECT EVERYTHING ELSE IN THE FOREST'
FAUNA & FLORA INTERNATIONAL

Venerated for its strength and longevity throughout human history, the
Asian Elephant is now in a precarious position, with little of its original
habitat left. Elephants need large, intact areas of forest to survive. Across
its range, forest is increasingly fragmented by human populations, bringing
it into more frequent conflict with people. Elephant bulls fall prey to ivory
poachers; others are killed for meat or body parts
for traditional medicines. Still others are domesticated as beasts of burden.

Fauna & Flora International (FFI) and its partners are working in
Cambodia and Indonesia, where large areas of habitat still remain.
Working with governments and communities, FFI is protecting the
forests for elephants and a host of other endangered species. As well
as monitoring herds, patrolling and preventing trade in elephant parts,
FFI is developing alternative livelihoods for communities that use
domesticated elephants, and is responding to human-elephant conflicts.

COMMON NAME: Asian Elephant

SCIENTIFIC NAME: *Elephas maximus*

SIZE: Up to 3m at the shoulder.

STATUS: Endangered.

POPULATION: Global population
estimates are of between 40,000
to 50,000, but a lack of reliable
up-to-date data suggests that
this figure could actually be much
lower, with possibly only 30,000
animals remaining in the wild.

LIFESPAN: Believed to be capable
of living up to 70 years.

RANGE: Discontinuously in Indian
sub-continent and South-east Asia,
south to Indonesia.

THREATS: Habitat loss and
fragmentation; poaching for ivory
and body parts; retribution killing
for destruction of property and
crops; and capture for domestication.

FAUNA & FLORA INTERNATIONAL   WHAT YOU CAN DO...

- Support FFI's work to protect Asian Elephants by emailing info@fauna-flora.org, or by visiting
  www.fauna-flora.org.

- Never buy ivory, even if it appears to be antique. Help reduce forest clearance by only purchasing
  Forest Stewardship Council (FSC)-certified wood products, recycling and using recycled materials.

AZRAQ KILLIFISH

'THE FIRST ALARM BELLS STARTED RINGING IN 1989 WHEN THE SPECIES WAS NOTICED TO BE IN DANGER OF SUFFERING FROM THE EFFECTS OF LOW WATER LEVELS'
ROYAL SOCIETY FOR THE CONSERVATION OF NATURE

Discovered just 30 years ago and found only in a single place, the Azraq wetland in Jordan, the Azraq Killifish is highly endangered. The first alarm bells started ringing in 1989 when the species was noticed to be in danger of suffering from the effects of low water levels, and in the following years its unique habitats continued to dry up.

To make matters worse, five alien species were introduced to the fish's wetland habitat, and these new species have been steadily out-competing the Killifish for food and breeding grounds, putting the little fish on the very brink of disappearance.

All is not quite lost, however: an ambitious project led by the Royal Society for the Conservation of Nature (RSCN) in Jordan has literally brought the fish back from the edge of extinction. In 2000, the few remaining individuals were collected and looked after in artificial yet ideal conditions, while their natural habitats were restored. By 2006, the population had recovered from a few hundred to a few thousand. It's a good start, but so much more still needs to be done to save this unique fish.

COMMON NAME: Azraq Killifish

SCIENTIFIC NAME: *Aphanius sirhani*

SIZE: From 2.5-5cm in length.

STATUS: Critically Endangered (not IUCN classified).

POPULATION: The fish is endemic to a small wetland in eastern Jordan known as Azraq wetland. Population of the species is estimated not to exceed a few thousand.

LIFESPAN: The Azraq killifish lives for one to three years, and longer in captivity.

RANGE: It only exists in Azraq wetland.

THREATS: Water shortage and fluctuation, in addition to the high competition with alien species for both food and breeding grounds.

بَرِّية الأردن
Wild Jordan
Helping Nature...Helping People

الجمعية الملكية
لحماية الطبيعة
RSCN
نساعد الطبيعة... نساعد الناس

WHAT YOU CAN DO...

- You can help the Azraq Killifish by donating to the Royal Society for the Conservation of Nature. Visit www.rscn.org.jo.

- Find out about the extraordinary biodiversity of Jordan by visiting the Royal Society for the Conservation of Nature's website, www.rscn.org.jo.

BARBARY MACAQUE

'POPULAR AS A TOURIST ATTRACTION IN GIBRALTAR, BUT MISUNDERSTOOD AND THEREFORE VULNERABLE IN THE WILD'
GONHS

You may be familiar with Europe's only wild monkeys, the famous 'Rock Apes' of Gibraltar. They are in fact Barbary Macaques, which are monkeys, the only macaques found outside Asia. Asiatic Macaques include the Rhesus and Long-tailed Macaques that, like the Barbaries in Gibraltar, are tourist attractions in the temples of India and South-east Asia.

In Gibraltar, the tradition of direct feeding of titbits by tourists has a negative impact on the health of the macaques and preconditions them to becoming urbanised and coming into conflict with the human population.

In the wild they are found as scattered groups of up to 70 in forests in the Rif and Atlas mountains of Morocco, and in open rocky habitats in both coastal Morocco and Algeria. They feed on a variety of plant material, including fruits, shoots, leaves and roots, as well as some invertebrates.

Changes in land use and other pressures from humans threaten in particular the wild Moroccan population.

COMMON NAME: Barbary Macaque

SCIENTIFIC NAME: *Macaca sylvanus*

SIZE: Up to 75cm height.

STATUS: Vulnerable.

POPULATION: There are about 240 living on Gibraltar, probably introduced from Morocco at least 200 years ago. The total population in north Africa is no more than 10,000.

LIFESPAN: Up to 25 years, probably less in a truly wild state.

RANGE: Formerly found throughout most of north Africa, they now only occur in Morocco and Algeria, as well as Gibraltar.

THREATS: Habitat degradation and loss, especially in the Middle Atlas, where overgrazing by domestic animals and difficulty in accessing water points due to increasing human pressure is reducing the quality of the habitat. This is causing them to damage cedars through the eating of bark, making them unpopular among the human population. There is also the problem of the capture of macaque infants for sale as pets in southern Europe.

WHAT YOU CAN DO...

- Enquire about ecotourism trips to Morocco with an emphasis on natural habitats and seeing the macaques in the wild. This will increase their value to the local community.

- Find out more about the work of The Gibraltar Ornithological & Natural History Society in Gibraltar and Morocco by visiting www.gonhs.org.

BASKING SHARK

'THE BASKING SHARK IS THE SECOND LARGEST FISH IN OUR OCEANS. THE PROTECTION OF FRAGILE MARINE HABITATS IS VITAL TO ENSURE A HEALTHY MARINE ENVIRONMENT THAT CAN SUPPORT THESE GENTLE GIANTS'
THE WILDLIFE TRUSTS

Basking Sharks are seriously threatened by overfishing – they were traditionally caught for their vast livers, but are now a target of the shark-fin-soup trade. It's thought that Basking Shark populations have decreased by 80% since the 1950s.

The Basking Shark feeds close to the surface of the water, swimming with its mouth wide open. Hundreds of tons of water flow into that wide gape every hour, from which the shark filters the plankton and other small invertebrates that it feeds on.

The Wildlife Trusts are working with fishermen, researchers, politicians and local people towards a vision of 'Living Seas', where marine wildlife thrives. This work has recently had a massive boost with the passing of the Marine and Coastal Access Act, promising sustainable development of the UK's marine environment.

Marine Protected Areas are sites where human activities are restricted to varying degrees. They are a tried and tested means of safeguarding important habitats and wildlife – protecting the wildlife within their boundaries and allowing nature to recover and thrive.

COMMON NAME: Basking Shark

SCIENTIFIC NAME: *Cetorhinus maximus*

SIZE: Average length 6-8m.

STATUS: Classified as Vulnerable on the IUCN Red List, listed under CITES Appendix II and classified as a Priority Species in the UK Biodiversity Action Plan.

POPULATION: Total numbers are unknown, but thought to be small and declining. Their long lifespan, slow maturity and low reproduction rate leave them vulnerable to overfishing and other threats.

LIFESPAN: Averaging around 50 years, but thought to be up to 100 years.

RANGE: Found in oceans across the world. Most commonly encountered in the UK along the west coast, particularly the south west of England and western Scottish islands.

THREATS: Boat strikes, entanglement in fishing nets and other human disturbance. Globally they are also threatened by the shark-fin trade and the effects of climate change on the availability and distribution of plankton.

WHAT YOU CAN DO...

- Support our call for Marine Protected Areas. Find out more at www.wildlifetrusts.org/living-seas.

- Report your sightings. The Wildlife Trusts is one of many organisations that help to monitor Basking Shark sightings around the UK. Photos are particularly important to aid identification of individual sharks, improving understanding of shark movements and numbers around our shores. Visit www.wildlifetrusts.org/living-seas.

- Join your local Wildlife Trust. The Wildlife Trusts is a partnership of 47 local Wildlife Trusts across the UK. To find your local Trust, visit www.wildlifetrusts.org/your-local-trust.

BECHSTEIN'S BAT

'BATS HAVE SUFFERED MAJOR DECLINES FROM HUMAN ACTIVITIES THAT HAVE CAUSED HABITATS TO BE DESTROYED AND THE INSECTS THEY FEED ON TO BECOME SCARCE'

BAT CONSERVATION TRUST

There are around 1,100 species of bat worldwide, making up about one-fifth of all mammals, yet relatively little is known about many of these incredible animals and at least 20% are threatened with extinction. Bats inspire strong passions, from great enthusiasm to fear and misunderstanding.

The Bechstein's Bat is one of Europe and the UK's rarest and most secretive bat species. It depends heavily on mature deciduous woodland for its survival; roosting in woodpecker holes and crevices in trees, and feeding on woodland insects, which it hunts using the specialised sense of echolocation.

Its preference for living in mature woodlands means that the Bechstein's Bat has suffered greatly from land use change that has caused extensive loss and fragmentation of woodland. Sensitive management of remaining mature woodland and measures to protect and connect woodlands are essential for the conservation of this species.

COMMON NAME: Bechstein's Bat

SCIENTIFIC NAME: *Myotis bechsteinii*

SIZE: Length 45-55mm, wingspan 250-300mm.

STATUS: Near-threatened

POPULATION: The exact worldwide population of the Bechstein's Bat is not known. However, we do know that the Bechstein's Bat has gone from being one of the commonest UK species to one of the rarest, due largely to the destruction of ancient woodland that once covered much of the UK. It is now thought to number as few as 1,500 individuals.

LIFESPAN: Bechstein's Bats have been recorded as living up to 21 years.

RANGE: The Bechstein's Bat is widespread, yet rare, across continental Europe.

THREATS: Destruction of ancient woodland, inappropriate woodland management resulting in loss of roost trees and reduced insect biodiversity, landscape fragmentation through removal of hedgerows, thereby diminishing connectivity between woodland areas.

Bat Conservation Trust WHAT YOU CAN DO...

- Support the work of the Bat Conservation Trust in conserving this and other bat species by becoming a member. Find out more online by visiting www.bats.org.uk.

- Take part in the National Bat Monitoring Programme to help track the progress of the UK's bat populations. You don't need to be an expert. Visit www.bats.org.uk.

BLACK POPLAR

'WITHOUT THE HELP OF LOCAL COMMUNITIES, BRITAIN'S RAREST NATIVE TREE COULD DISAPPEAR'
THE CONSERVATION VOLUNTEERS

The native Black Poplar (*Populus nigra* var. *betulifolia*) was once a common and distinctive sight on the UK's flood plains and rivers, finding its way into many famous works of art, including John Constable's *The Hay Wain*. Its springy timber, prized as a heat and shock absorber, was also widely used in industry. Applications included brake blocks, railway carriage buffers, floorboards, rifle butts and wagon bottoms.

Yet since the 17th century there has been a spectacular decline in populations due to the drainage of flood plains and subsequent loss of habitat. Few people have now ever heard of the tree or would be able to recognise it (they often confuse the Black Poplar with non-native hybrids). There are now only 7,000 trees nationally.

The tree's plight is compounded by its dioecious nature, with male and female catkins growing on different trees. In Norfolk, for example, the situation is precarious: of 70 Black Poplars spread across the county, only one is female. Climate changes, habitat loss and increasing distance between trees mean there is little chance for natural seed pollination and germination. Here volunteers supported by The Conservation Volunteers have acted as 'nursemaids' for a batch of cuttings taken from identified existing specimens. These have been planted at allotment sites offering open and moist conditions ideally suited to the young trees. This has produced a stock of rooted clones that are now being planted across the county.

COMMON NAME: Black Poplar

SCIENTIFIC NAME: *Populus nigra* var. *betulifolia*

SIZE: Up to 30m in height.

STATUS: Britain's rarest native tree.

POPULATION: 7,000 across UK and the Republic of Ireland.

LIFESPAN: Over 200 years.

RANGE: Britain, Ireland, Northern, France and parts of Western Germany.

THREATS: Loss of habitat due to drainage, lack of genetic diversity, ageing population (few planted since the 1850s) and lack of recognition.

WHAT YOU CAN DO...

- Help The Conservation Volunteers reclaim green spaces. Go online to tcv.org.uk, or send a donation to the Conservation Volunteers, Sedum House, Mallard Way, Doncaster DN4 8DB. £10 can support one child to explore and learn about nature. £20 can provide tools for a new conservation volunteer.

BLACK RHINOCEROS

'BETWEEN 1960 AND 1995, THE POPULATION OF
BLACK RHINO DECLINED BY AN ESTIMATED 97.6%'
SAVE THE RHINO INTERNATIONAL

Having been the most numerous of the world's rhino species, once numbering around 850,000, the population of Black Rhino declined by an estimated 97.6% between 1960 and 1995, with numbers falling to 2,410, mainly as a result of large-scale poaching. Since then, numbers have been steadily increasing at a continental level, doubling to 4,880 by the end of 2010. However, there are still 90% fewer than three generations ago.

Historically, there were four subspecies of Black Rhino, but in 2011, the Western Black Rhino (subspecies *longipes*) was formally declared extinct. Poaching remains the biggest threat to the Black Rhino's survival, with demand for rhino horn from Asian countries (particularly Vietnam and China) surging in recent years. The high prices fetched for rhino horns have led to the involvement of ruthless criminal syndicates. In Asia, rhino horn is now being used as a status symbol and for non-traditional uses, such as the treatment of cancer and hangovers, despite no clinical evidence of its effectiveness.

Effective field protection and biological management of rhino populations have been critical to the recent increase in Black Rhino numbers. To reduce the current poaching crisis, strong political will, global cooperation and efforts to reduce the demand for illegal rhino horn are needed. For long-term survival it is also important to integrate local communities into conservation efforts.

COMMON NAME: Black Rhinoceros

SCIENTIFIC NAME: *Diceros bicornis*

SIZE: 2.8-3.8m in length.

STATUS: Critically Endangered.

POPULATION: 5,055 as at December 2012.

LIFESPAN: Black Rhinos live on average 30-40 years in the wild and 35-45+ years in captivity.

RANGE: Black Rhinos are mainly found in South Africa, Namibia, Kenya and Zimbabwe. There are smaller populations in Botswana, Tanzania, Malawi, Swaziland and Zambia, with possible individuals in Angola and Mozambique.

THREATS: Poaching of rhinos' horns for traditional (and more recently new non-traditional) use in Chinese medicine. Other threats include political conflict, civil unrest and habitat destruction.

WHAT YOU CAN DO...

- Become a member of Save the Rhino International and help raise money to support rhino programmes across Africa. Visit www.savetherhino.org or telephone +44 (0) 20 7357 7474.

- Sign up to receive Save the Rhino's monthly e-newsletter RhiNEWS to keep up to date with rhino issues, events and how to become involved. Email 'subscribe' to info@savetherhino.org or visit the website above.

BLUE-GREY TAILDROPPER

'DESPITE THEIR UNASSUMING APPEARANCE, THESE SLUGS ARE A PART OF OUR NATURAL HERITAGE AND IT IS OUR RESPONSIBILITY TO CARE FOR THEM'
HABITAT ACQUISITION TRUST

Among fallen leaves at the edge of oak meadows on Canada's southern Vancouver Island lives a small bright blue slug that feeds mainly on mushrooms and truffles. The Blue-grey Taildropper is only a few centimetres long and ranges in colour from typical slug grey to a surprising bright blue. As its name suggests, the taildropper can 'drop', or autotomise, its tail to distract predators while it makes a slow getaway. Over several months, the tail can grow back.

The Blue-grey Taildropper is not to blame for eating lettuce seedlings and wants little to do with the garden. Preferring to live among leaf litter in moist, cool and shady spots, it feeds heavily on mycorrhizal fungi that are symbiotic with tree roots, and helps to spread the spores of these beneficial mushrooms throughout the forest.

Unfortunately for the Blue-grey Taildropper, only 5% of its natural habitat in oak meadows remains, and even that is being rapidly lost to development and degraded by invasive plants and animals. Furthermore, many gardeners and homeowners, frustrated with slugs dining on their veggies, resort to slug baits. These baits don't discriminate between harmless forest slugs and damaging garden invaders, and often contain toxic chemicals that can kill small mammals, snakes and many other animals too.

COMMON NAME:
Blue-grey Taildropper
SCIENTIFIC NAME:
Prophysaon coeruleum
SIZE: 2-3cm in length.
STATUS: Endangered (listed by the Committee on the Status of Endangered Wildlife in Canada).
POPULATION: Unknown, but very small.
LIFESPAN: Unknown, but possibly just one year.
RANGE: In Canada, known from only a few sites all within 30km of Victoria.
THREATS: Blue-grey Taildroppers are losing their habitat to development, and populations are increasingly fragmented. They may also be inadvertently poisoned by gardeners using slug baits.

HAT WHAT YOU CAN DO...

- Leave fallen logs and sloughed-off bark as they fall as they provide hiding places for the Blue-grey Taildropper, and encourage native plants and shrubs that are habitat for the slugs, as well as for a variety of other wildlife.

- Avoid using slug baits, especially methaldehyde-based bait. Slug baits use toxic chemicals to kill slugs, but they kill all slugs, and other animals, too, such as snakes, which can get poisoned when they eat slugs.

- Sign up for Habitat Acquisition Trust's newsletter to find out more about what we are doing to conserve and restore habitat for the Blue-grey Taildropper by visiting www.hat.bc.ca.

BLUE-THROATED MACAW

'THE POPULATION IS EXTREMELY SMALL WITH FEWER THAN 125 KNOWN BIRDS IN THE WILD'
WORLD PARROT TRUST

Parrots are beautiful, charismatic and many have the ability to talk. Sadly, this also puts them in serious danger of extinction, with capture in large numbers for the bird trade adding to the problem caused by habitat loss.

Their beauty and intelligence makes Blue-throated Macaws much sought after as pets. Listed as Critically Endangered, their population underwent a rapid reduction due to trapping for trade during the 1980s and it is now extremely small and dispersed over a large area. All known breeding sites are on cattle ranches – land on which forest is often cleared for pasture, and trees suitable for nests felled for fence posts and fuel.

The World Parrot Trust has been researching and managing the wild population in a large area for more than 10 years, and has made important discoveries about the Blue-throated Macaw's habitat, its unique nesting ecology and the issues limiting its recovery. The project has developed into a complex conservation programme, and key factors include the protection and management of wild nests, the restoration of select habitat areas affected by cattle ranching, and the education of local stakeholders in determining long-term land management strategies.

To ensure a rapid and healthy recovery of this rare macaw, the World Parrot Trust is establishing a captive breeding and release programme on protected land with the approval of the Bolivian government.

COMMON NAME: Blue-throated Macaw

SCIENTIFIC NAME: *Ara glaucogularis*

SIZE: Approx 85cm in length.

STATUS: CITES Appendix 1. Critically Endangered.

POPULATION: Several thousand in captivity, but fewer than 125 known birds in the wild.

LIFESPAN: At least 32 years.

RANGE: Bolivia.

THREATS: The population is extremely small, in tiny isolated groups, and declining as a result of trade and habitat loss.

WORLD PARROT TRUST WHAT YOU CAN DO...

- Support work for the Blue-throated Macaw by buying a Blue-throated Macaw T-shirt, available online at www.parrots.org.

- To help parrot conservation join the World Parrot Trust. Visit the website www.parrots.org, call 01736 751026 and join them on Facebook and Twitter.

BOTTLENOSE DOLPHIN

'BOTTLENOSE DOLPHINS CURRENTLY FACE MOUNTING THREATS TO THEIR SURVIVAL; ACTING TOMORROW MIGHT BE TOO LATE'
BORN FREE FOUNDATION

Overfishing for human consumption is bringing Bottlenose Dolphins into frequent contact and conflict with humans, increasing the potential that they will be killed as bycatch, as well as decreasing their available food sources. Pollution of marine habitats also adversely affects Bottlenose Dolphin populations and their prey species. However, many other threats also exist including live capture for captive facilities, hunting for human food or sport, and culling.

A long gestation period and the number of years taken to reach sexual maturity mean that Bottlenose Dolphins are particularly vulnerable to, and slow to recover from, adverse environmental conditions.

Every year more than 20,000 dolphins are slaughtered in Taiji, Japan, alone. Whole pods are rounded up by fishermen after which the most 'attractive' ones are caught and taken to captive facilities, and the rest are slaughtered and sold on for human consumption.

The Mediterranean and Black Sea populations have been declining for over 20 years. These threats may appear inconsequential when compared to the current population estimates, but when combined increase the possibility that this iconic species may disappear from parts of their current range if measures are not taken.

Born Free campaigns against the capture and keeping of dolphins in captive facilities. Recently it successfully rehabilitated and released two male Bottlenose Dolphins back to the wild after years in captive facilities in Turkey.

COMMON NAME: Bottlenose Dolphin

SCIENTIFIC NAME: *Tursiops truncatus*

SIZE: Body length can vary between 2.5 and 4 meters.

STATUS: Least Concern (IUCN Red List).

POPULATION: Estimated 600,000 worldwide and declining.

LIFESPAN: Between 48-57 years.

RANGE: Currently found in all tropical and temperate waters.

THREATS: Numerous, including incidental catch, live capture for captive facilities and environmental degradation. In some areas they are also hunted for human food or culled to protect fisheries.

WHAT YOU CAN DO...

- Joining the Born Free Foundation is the best way readers can support all our work and get more involved with the charity. To find out more about both Born Free and its various projects, please visit www.bornfree.org.uk. Charity number 1070906.

BROWN HYENA

'THIS CRYPTIC ANIMAL USUALLY LIVES AROUND US WITHOUT BEING NOTICED, BUT ONCE DETECTED, IT IS GENERALLY MISUNDERSTOOD AND THEREFORE IN DANGER'
BROWN HYENA RESEARCH PROJECT

Although Spotted Hyenas are well known to the public, not many people have ever seen a Brown Hyena or even know of their existence. These large African carnivores are predominantly scavengers, but also hunt seal pups along the Namib Desert coast.

Their sense of smell is extremely well developed and they can detect carcasses over great distances. However, the Brown Hyena's ability to find carrion quickly is one of its greatest problems. Outside protected areas, they are often found first at carcasses and hence blamed for killing livestock, resulting in their persecution.

Brown Hyena home range sizes vary depending on the distribution of food sources and can be as large as 1,500km². They cover vast distances at night, sometimes up to 40km. While travelling, they often have to cross roads and are frequently hit and killed by vehicles.

A lack of knowledge about Brown Hyenas within local communities also exposes the creatures to risks because they are feared and killed, or injured in snares.

COMMON NAME: Brown Hyena

SCIENTIFIC NAME: *Hyaena brunnea*

SIZE: Up to 140cm in length.

STATUS: International: Near-threatened. Namibia: Insufficiently Known (Vulnerable or Endangered).

POPULATION: The entire population is estimated at 5,000 to 8,000. animals. Namibia has a population of around 800 to 1,200 animals.

LIFESPAN: Lifespan of Brown Hyenas in the wild is unknown, but some wild animals reach ages of 16 years. They can reach over 20 years in captivity.

RANGE: Brown Hyenas occur in the southern African sub-region.

THREATS: Habitat destruction and fragmentation, human/carnivore conflict resulting in poisoning and trapping, road kills.

WHAT YOU CAN DO...

- Become a friend of the Brown Hyena Research Project. Send an e-mail to strandwolf@iway.na, with 'BHRP Friend' in the subject line. Friends receive our newsletter, and the donations and fees help to run the conservation projects in Namibia.

- Adopt or sponsor a Brown Hyena (email strandwolf@iway.na or visit www.strandwolf.org).

CHEETAH

'THE WORLD'S FASTEST LAND ANIMAL IS RUNNING OUT OF TIME'
CHEETAH CONSERVATION FUND

The sleek and long-legged Cheetah is losing its race for survival. Once a common animal found on five continents, the Cheetah is now an endangered species.

Loss of habitat, poaching, competition with large predators and ranchers, as well as its own loss of genetic variation, are killing off the remaining Cheetahs. Unfortunately, captive breeding efforts have not proven meaningful to the Cheetah's hopes of survival. The Cheetah needs a large expanse of land to survive, but with the growth of the human population, this area is becoming smaller and smaller.

The largest population of Cheetahs is in Namibia. Since the country's recent expansion, there was a drastic decline in Cheetah numbers in the 1980s, when the population was halved in just 10 years, leaving an estimated total of fewer than 2,500 animals.

Now, only humans can save the Cheetah from extinction.

COMMON NAME: Cheetah

SCIENTIFIC NAME: *Acinonyx jubatus*

SIZE: Up to 1.5m in length.

STATUS: Protected species in Namibia. Listed on CITES Appendix I. First listed on 1 July 1975.

POPULATION: About 10,000 Cheetahs remain in 23-24 African countries, and fewer than 70 survive in Iran. Namibia has the world's largest number of Cheetahs, with approximately 3,500 in the wild.

LIFESPAN: Studies have not been conducted in the wild on longevity; 8-12 years is average in captivity.

RANGE: Once found throughout Asia and Africa, the species is now mainly found in Africa.

THREATS: Decline in prey, loss of habitat, poaching, and indiscriminate trapping and shooting as a livestock predator threaten the survival of the Cheetah throughout its range.

WHAT YOU CAN DO...

- Become a member of the Cheetah Conservation Fund (CCF). Visit the CCF website at www.cheetah.org.

- You can sponsor or adopt a Cheetah cub or family, or simply make a donation to the CCF.

CHIMPANZEE

'BEING KILLED FOR BUSHMEAT, OUR NEAREST RELATIVES ARE GOING TO DISAPPEAR FOR EVER IF WE CAN'T STOP POACHING AND HABITAT DESTRUCTION'
PRO WILDLIFE

Chimpanzees are the species most similar to humans – both genetically and behaviourally. However, increased encroachment of humans into their habitat and poaching threaten their survival. Whereas Chimpanzees have always been hunted for consumption, the impact of hunting has become disastrous in recent years: growing human populations, combined with the opening up of formerly inaccessible areas (for example, through logging companies or for road construction), have resulted in a massive and increasing hunt.

Chimpanzees are especially sought after due to the relatively large amount of meat that a hunter can obtain with one single bullet. Furthermore, according to an old tradition, meat from great apes is supposed to be particularly healthy. Despite being protected legally, poaching has become a lucrative business and thousands of Chimpanzees are killed annually. Often, poachers kill all adults of a Chimpanzee group, whereas the surviving infants are sold as pets. Most of them suffer in chains or small cages.

COMMON NAME: Chimpanzee

SCIENTIFIC NAME: *Pan troglodytes*

SIZE: Up to 1.7m standing.

STATUS: Endangered.

POPULATION: There are four subspecies: the Western Chimpanzee (*P. t. verus*) with about 38,000 individuals; Nigeria Chimpanzee (*P. t. ellioti*) 6,000; Central Chimpanzee (*P. t. troglodytes*) 93,000; and Eastern Chimpanzee (*P. t. schweinfurthii*) 98,000.

LIFESPAN: Up to 60 years.

RANGE: Chimpanzees live in west and central Africa. The largest populations now exist in the Democratic Republic of Congo, Gabon and Cameroon.

THREATS: Populations have been reduced by more than two-thirds within the past three decades. Chimpanzeeanzees are mainly threatened by poaching for the bushmeat trade and deforestation, but also by diseases and capture as pets and for research.

PRO WILDLIFE

WHAT YOU CAN DO...

- Adopt a Chimpanzee (visit the website at www.prowildlife.de/en/adoption/adoption). The money raised helps Pro Wildlife to rescue primate orphans, run education programmes and fight habitat destruction and poaching.

- Write to the EU to halt timber imports from unsustainable logging: EU Environment Commissioner, Environment DG, European Commission, B-1049 Brussels, Belgium.

COMMON CRANE

'ALTHOUGH IT IS ONCE AGAIN INCREASING, THE UK'S SMALL POPULATION OF CRANES STILL NEEDS A LOT OF HELP'
PENSTHORPE CONSERVATION TRUST

Cranes were once a popular dish on the menu of the nobility, appearing on the heavily laden banquet tables of lords, archbishops and kings. However, the intensive hunting to which it was exposed proved to be unsustainable and the crane sadly disappeared from the British Isles. Four hundred years passed but in the late 20th century a small population became re-established in Norfolk. In between times the only remaining whisperings of how common the crane once was, had been the widespread use of 'cran', 'corn' and 'tran' (all words meaning crane in Old English and Norse) in the names of so many places across Britain.

During the crane's long absence the British landscape changed and habitat loss, together with large-scale intensification of agriculture, had a detrimental effect on so many birds; reducing food availability, as well as safe roosting and breeding sites away from human interference. Although it is once again increasing, the UK's small population of cranes still needs a lot of help. The Great Crane Project aims to re-establish cranes in suitable wetland habitats across the UK, initially on the Somerset Levels and Moors. With a growing population at several sites across the UK and a target of 100 young birds to be released in Somerset by 2015, we're confident that the long-forgotten, spine-tingling bugling of cranes gathering at their evening roosts is back for good!

COMMON NAME: Common Crane
SCIENTIFIC NAME: *Grus grus*
SIZE: Up to 130cm in height with a wingspan of up to 240cm.
STATUS: Amber-listed in the UK.
POPULATION: Global 360,000 to 370,000; UK 50 to100 (plus a growing number of birds from the Great Crane Project reintroduction and increased breeding success).
LIFESPAN: Up to 14 years.
RANGE: North-Eastern Europe; Northern and Central Asia.
THREATS: Habitat loss and encroachment, nest predation and disturbance.

WHAT YOU CAN DO...

- Visit and support the Pensthorpe Conservation Trust in Norfolk (www.pensthorpetrust.org.uk), as well as WWT and RSPB sites around Britain; and support the work of the Great Crane Project (www.thegreatcraneproject.org.uk).

COMMON DORMOUSE

'A HEALTHY, WELL-CONNECTED NATURAL ENVIRONMENT IS CRUCIAL TO HELP POPULATIONS RECOVER AND RETURN TO THEIR TRADITIONAL RANGE'

CHESHIRE WILDLIFE TRUST

Cheshire Wildlife Trust, in partnership with Chester Zoo and the People's Trust for Endangered Species reintroduced these rare mammals into a south Cheshire woodland during the mid-1990s, almost 80 years since the last wild Cheshire Dormouse had been seen. Once widespread in its favoured woodland habitat, remaining UK Dormouse populations are now scattered and isolated, due to forest and hedgerow destruction.

Almost 200 nesting boxes were installed in the chosen woodland, providing both an important refuge and a way for researchers to track the progress of the scheme. More than 15 years on, the scheme remains the first research monitoring project on a reintroduced population of Dormice and in recent years has embraced microchip technology. The team are now looking into further innovations including using trained conservation dogs to help locate wild nests that may be beyond the scope of researchers.

COMMON NAME: Common (or Hazel) Dormouse

SCIENTIFIC NAME: *Muscardinus avellanarius*

SIZE: 6-9 cm in length.

STATUS: Classified as a Priority Species in the UK Biodiversity Action Plan.

POPULATION: Numbers have declined dramatically over the 20th century. The total UK population is now estimated at around 45,000.

LIFESPAN: Up to five years in the wild.

RANGE: The Common Dormouse's traditional range in the UK has halved in recent decades. It is now found mainly in the south of England, with small populations across the Midlands, Wales and in northern counties such as Northumberland, Cumbria and Cheshire.

THREATS: Habitat loss, particularly of traditionally coppiced woodland, has resulted in the widespread decline of Dormice across the UK. Careful habitat management is required to provide a diverse range of food plants and corridors for movement.

Cheshire WHAT YOU CAN DO...

- Become a conservation volunteer. Sympathetic habitat management is crucial to ensure the UK's landscapes meet the needs of wildlife. For Dormice, this involves regular woodland clearance work and coppicing, as well as nest box maintenance and monitoring. Find out more at www.wildlifetrusts.org/discover-learn/volunteering.

- Adopt a Dormouse. Many Wildlife Trusts have species adoption schemes. Find out more at www.wildlifetrusts.org/how-you-can-help/adopt-species/adopt-dormouse.

- Join your local Wildlife Trust. The Wildlife Trusts is a partnership of 47 local Wildlife Trusts across the UK. To find your local Trust, visit www.wildllifetrusts.org/your-local-trust.

COMMON HIPPOPOTAMUS

'ONCE REGARDED AS WIDESPREAD, THE COMMON HIPPOPOTAMUS IS NOW AT RISK OF EXTINCTION DUE TO HABITAT LOSS, POACHING AND THE EFFECTS OF CLIMATE CHANGE'
FRIENDS OF CONSERVATION

Charismatic and social animals, Hippopotamuses or 'river horses' are gregarious creatures, found in African wetlands, swamps and rivers. Unfortunately, with the growth in the human population, hippo habitat – in common with that of many other species – is being encroached upon.

Changes to the climate and increased agricultural development mean that water courses are drying up or being diverted. The declining hippo population is further threatened by poaching, with their ivory teeth being sought after, for example, in the manufacture of souvenirs.

Friends of Conservation (FOC) works in Kenya's greater Mara region; offering practical support to local communities and encouraging the sustainable use of natural resources.

FOC is involved in and funds programmes, including wildlife monitoring, anti-poaching activities and conservation education; runs workshops on business skills and health awareness; and advocates the use of renewable fuels to help conserve wildlife habitat.

COMMON NAME: Common Hippopotamus

SCIENTIFIC NAME: *Hippopotamus amphibius*

SIZE: Up to 5m in length.

STATUS: Vulnerable.

POPULATION: Several of the subpopulation groups in west Africa contain fewer than 100 individuals, well below the minimum considered to be viable. The total population is estimated at between 125,000 and 150,000.

LIFESPAN: Males reach maturity between 6-14 years and females between 7-15 years. Their lifespan is between 40-50 years.

RANGE: Found throughout sub-Saharan Africa with some sizeable populations in certain countries, for example Zambia and Mozambique. Overall, however, the species is in decline.

THREATS: Loss of grazing land due to human settlement, the effects of climate change on habitat, and poaching for its ivory teeth, meat and skin.

FOC
FRIENDS OF CONSERVATION

WHAT YOU CAN DO...

- By becoming a member of FOC you can help support endangered wildlife and threatened habitats worldwide. Please visit www.foc-uk.com for more information.

- When travelling, consider offsetting the carbon dioxide emissions that contribute to climate change by donating to FOC programmes, which aim to mitigate these effects, such as reforestation, or encourage the use of alternative energies, including solar power. Find out more at www.foc-uk.com.

CORAL REEFS

'CORAL REEFS ARE AMONGST THE OLDEST AND LARGEST LIVING STRUCTURES ON EARTH. CLIMATE CHANGE, POLLUTION AND OVEREXPLOITATION ARE SERIOUSLY THREATENING THEIR SURVIVAL'
BIOSPHERE EXPEDITIONS

Corals are anthozoans, the largest class of organisms within the phylum Cnidaria (corals, hydras, jellyfish and Sea Anemones), comprising over 6,000 known species. A group called stony corals is primarily responsible for laying the foundations of, and building up, reef structures by secreting calcium carbonate skeletons. Different species of coral build structures of various sizes and shapes ('brain corals', 'fan corals', etc), creating amazing diversity and complexity in the coral reef ecosystem. Coral reefs form some of the world's most productive ecosystems, providing complex and varied marine habitats that support very high biodiversity. Coral reefs deliver ecosystem services to tourism, fisheries and coastline protection. Their global economic value has been estimated at as much as £250 (US$375) billion per year. Many small islands would simply not exist without their reefs to protect them. But coral reefs are dying around the world. Coral mining, pollution, overfishing, blast fishing, disease and the digging of canals are localised threats to coral ecosystems. Broader threats are sea temperature rise, sea level rise and pH changes from ocean acidification, all associated with global climate change. Today the majority of reefs are threatened or severely degraded. By the 2030s, 90% of reefs are expected to be at risk; by 2050, all coral reefs will be in danger. Through research and conservation work, Biosphere Expeditions and many other organisations are working on turning the tide.

COMMON NAME: Coral reefs

SCIENTIFIC NAME: *Coral polyps* belong to a group of animals known as *Cnidaria*, which also includes sea anemones and jellyfish

STATUS: 10% of the world's coral reefs are dead, about 60% are at risk, particularly in South-east Asia, where 80% of reefs are endangered.

POPULATION: Coral reefs are estimated to cover 284,300 sqkm or just under 0.1% of the oceans' surface area.

LIFESPAN: Most coral reefs were formed after the last glacial period about 10,000 years ago.

RANGE: Tropical seas within 30 degrees either side of the equator.

THREATS: Climate change, pollution, human impact, overfishing/exploitation.

WHAT YOU CAN DO...

- Join a coral reef research and conservation expedition. Biosphere Expeditions run these in Oman, Malaysia, the Maldives and Honduras – www.biosphere-expeditions.org.

- Join Reef Check www.reefcheck.org, an international conservation organisation dedicated to reef conservation.

CORNCOCKLE

'MODERN HERBICIDE USE HAS DRIVEN THIS ONCE WIDESPREAD CORNFIELD FLOWER TO NEAR EXTINCTION IN THE UK'

PLANTLIFE

The story of Corncockle is the story of arable farming in Britain. Attractive and unmistakable, its single flowers of a deep pink colour have been present in our arable fields since the Iron Age. Corncockle was once common as part of species-rich cornfield communities.

However, along with other threatened arable flowers such as the cornflower, it now faces extinction. Apart from occasional appearances after deep-buried seed is brought to the surface, Corncockle is now rarely seen in arable fields. Its downfall came about because its large, black seeds taste so bitter. This meant that when the corn and rye crops were milled for flour, the resulting bread was inedible. The development of seed-cleaning technologies at the end of the 19th century and the application of modern herbicides in the 20th century sealed its fate and our countryside has lost, perhaps for ever, the tall, bright flowers with their delicate, purple-streaked petals.

COMMON NAME: Corncockle

SCIENTIFIC NAME: *Agrostemma githago*

SIZE: Up to 100cm.

STATUS: On the 'waiting list' for the Vascular Plant Red Data List for Great Britain.

POPULATION: Although widespread as an introduction, there are only one or two sites where it survives as an original, ancient cornfield plant.

LIFESPAN: An annual species, so dies at the end of the season. However, its buried seeds can remain dormant for a long time.

RANGE: Native range uncertain, perhaps eastern Mediterranean; spread with cultivation throughout temperate and southern Europe, and other areas.

THREATS: Modern farming practices, particularly seed-cleaning processes and the application of herbicide and fertiliser on arable land.

Plantlife WHAT YOU CAN DO...

- Adopt a flower (visit the website www.plantlife.org.uk). The money raised supports Plantlife's work to rescue wild flowers on the brink of extinction and to conserve landscapes of exceptional botanical importance.

- Be aware that Corncockle seeds found in commercial wildflower seed mixes are not sourced from the UK and the resulting plants will have a different genetic identity. Enjoy them in your garden but please do not scatter these seeds into the wider countryside.

DALL'S PORPOISE

'SINCE 1980 MORE THAN 460,000 DALL'S PORPOISES HAVE BEEN KILLED IN JAPAN IN THE WORLD'S LARGEST CETACEAN HUNT'
ENVIRONMENTAL INVESTIGATION AGENCY

The international moratorium on commercial whaling, implemented in 1986, saved the great whales from extinction. It did not, however, protect smaller cetaceans and one stocky little black and white porpoise still suffers an appalling annual slaughter.

The Dall's Porpoise is an energetic swimmer. Capable of speeds up to 55kph, it is the only porpoise frequently observed riding the bow-waves of ships. Since 1980, more than 460,000 have been killed in Japan in the world's largest cetacean hunt.

Although temporarily suspended due to the March 2011 tsunami, which hit the north-east coast of Japan, the hunt resumed in 2012 with hunters chasing a dangerously high annual quota of 14,055.

In the past, hunters have targeted nursing females because they travel slowly to protect their calves and are easier to catch. The calves are left to starve and the loss of females upsets the sex ratio in this population, which is now at risk. The Scientific Committee of the International Whaling Commission (IWC) has expressed 'extreme concern' over this 'clearly unsustainable' hunt, yet Japan wants to restore commercial killing of all the world's whales.

COMMON NAME: Dall's Porpoise
SCIENTIFIC NAME: *Phocoenoides dalli*
SIZE: Up to 2.3m in length.
STATUS: Lower Risk – conservation dependent.
POPULATION: The targeted populations are thought to number 443,000 individuals.
LIFESPAN: 16 years.
RANGE: Endemic to the North Pacific.
THREATS: Unsustainable hunting by harpoon; driftnet bycatch; loss of prey due to expansion of squid fishing; pollution.

WHAT YOU CAN DO...

- The Environmental Investigation Agency's (EIA) ongoing investigations and campaigning have been a persuasive influence at the IWC. Support EIA's Dall's Porpoise Campaign by making a donation at www.eia-international.org.

- Become a regular EIA donor and receive the twice-yearly newsletter 'Investigator'; visit www.eia-international.org/donate for information.

DELHI SANDS FLOWER-LOVING FLY

'THE DELHI SANDS FLOWER-LOVING FLY IS A FLAGSHIP FOR THE WHOLE DELHI SANDS ECOSYSTEM. AS LONG AS THE FLY STAYS AFLOAT, THE REST OF ITS HABITAT DOES, TOO'
THE XERCES SOCIETY

The Delhi Sands Flower-loving Fly is a giant in the fly world. It is more than 2.5cm long, with beautiful green eyes and a craving for nectar. It is also native to the irreplaceable – and rapidly disappearing – Delhi Sands ecosystem in southern California. Because of urban development, researchers estimate only 2-3% of the fly's sand dune habitat remains.

Scientists have called the Delhi Sands Flower-loving Fly a flagship species for the whole Delhi Sands ecosystem. Protecting the Delhi fly's habitat will preserve important open space that is habitat to a variety of wildlife. We may not know what specific role the Delhi fly plays in these dunes, but, as the ecologist Aldo Leopold said: 'To keep every cog and wheel is the first precaution of intelligent tinkering.' We must act now if we are to save the Delhi Sands Flower-loving Fly – our unique natural heritage – from vanishing for ever.

COMMON NAME: Delhi Sands Flower-loving Fly

SCIENTIFIC NAME: *Rhaphiomidas terminatus abdominalis*

SIZE: Average length 25mm.

STATUS: Critically Endangered.

POPULATION: The Delhi Sands Flower-loving Fly is only known from 12 sites and less than 3% of its habitat remains.

LIFESPAN: Adults live two to three weeks. Larvae may be picked up by ants and taken to the ant nest where they are fed and tended as ant brood and live throughout the rest of the year.

RANGE: Can only be found in the Delhi Sands ecosystem in southern California, US.

THREATS: Development of the Delhi Sands Flower-loving Fly's habitat for housing developments, roads and shopping malls.

THE XERCES SOCIETY
FOR INVERTEBRATE CONSERVATION

WHAT YOU CAN DO...

- Contact the US Fish and Wildlife Service and ask that it prioritises protection of the Delhi Sands Flower-loving Fly's ecosystem. US Fish and Wildlife Service, Carlsbad Fish and Wildlife Office, 2730 Loker Ave West, Carlsbad, CA 92008.

- Join The Xerces Society for Invertebrate Conservation and help it to protect the Delhi Sands Flower-loving Fly and other invertebrates at www.xerces.org.

DISTINGUISHED JUMPING SPIDER

'THIS SPIDER HAS ONLY BEEN FOUND AT TWO SITES IN THE UK, BOTH POTENTIALLY THREATENED BY DEVELOPMENT'

BUGLIFE – THE INVERTEBRATE CONSERVATION TRUST

The Distinguished Jumping Spider has a large pair of eyes at the front of its head, providing excellent vision for hunting prey. Their keen eyesight also plays a part in courtship, during which males undertake elaborate dance to woo a female (and avoid being eaten!).

The spider is associated with former industrial sites, known as brownfield sites, where the females place their egg cocoons inside the bubble holes of clinker (an industrial waste product). Brownfield is undervalued and is under massive development pressure – especially in the Thames Gateway – and is being prioritised for development in Planning Policy.

This Distinguished Jumping Spider and many other species associated with brownfield sites, such as the Streaked Bombardier Beetle, are threatened by development. Since 2008, more than half of the sites Buglife identified as valuable invertebrate habitats have been lost or are due to be developed.

COMMON NAME: Distinguished Jumping Spider

SCIENTIFIC NAME: *Sitticus distinguendus*

SIZE: Average length 6mm.

STATUS: 2007 UKBAP and Section 41 of the NERC Act (2006).

POPULATION: Recorded at two sites in the UK, two males and one female were found at West Thurrock Marsh, Essex, a former power station, in 2003, and a single female was found in 2004 at a cement factory flue-ash site at Swanscombe Marshes in north Kent.

LIFESPAN: Little is known about the life cycle, both adults and juveniles have been found at the same time of year, suggesting the lifespan is spread over at least two years.

RANGE: Although found in 11 European countries, it is evidently rare and threatened in most areas due to habitat loss and fragmentation.

THREATS: Only known from two sites – both are subject to building development.

WHAT YOU CAN DO...

- Join Buglife – Buglife is the only organisation in Europe devoted to the conservation of all invertebrates, and it is active in saving rare bugs, snails, bees, spiders, beetles and many more. Visit www.buglife.org.uk.

- Volunteer at a Buglife practical habitat management work party to ensure that brownfield habitats are kept in favourable condition for bugs. You could help create a bee bank or remove scrub to reveal bare ground – ideal for basking beetles. Visit www.buglife.org.uk/volunteering.

DRILL

'RELATIVELY UNKNOWN, DRILLS ARE CURRENTLY THE
HIGHEST-PRIORITY AFRICAN PRIMATE FOR CONSERVATION'
THE AFRICAN CONSERVATION FOUNDATION

The Drill, an endangered forest-dwelling baboon, lives in the rainforests of western Cameroon, Nigeria and Bioko Island. Drills prefer primary undisturbed forests and are rarely seen in open country, away from the shelter of trees.

Male Drills can be distinguished from male Mandrills, their close relations, by the absence of bright red and blue facial skin.

Little is known about the ecology or behaviour of Drills in the wild, but we do know that the conservation status of this species is precarious due to human pressure. Forest destruction and fragmentation throughout its highly restricted range is causing local extinction of the species and of other primates. These areas are also centres of high endemism – many of these species are not found anywhere else.

In addition, Drills are hunted extensively for their meat, which is being sold at local markets.

COMMON NAME: Drill

SCIENTIFIC NAME: *Mandrillus leucophaeus*

SIZE: Up to 70cm in length.

STATUS: Endangered.

POPULATION: Not entirely known, but not considered to be common.

LIFESPAN: Drills in captivity can live up to 45 years, but their lifespan in the wild is unknown.

RANGE: Lowland, coastal and montane rainforests (up to 1,000m) of western Cameroon, Nigeria and Bioko Island (Equatorial Guinea).

THREATS: Habitat loss and fragmentation due to deforestation, as well as hunting for the bushmeat trade.

AFRICAN CONSERVATION FOUNDATION
WHAT YOU CAN DO...

- Join The African Conservation Foundation (ACF), buy wildlife art through www.artsavingwildlife.org or make a donation. The funds raised help the ACF protect drills and mandrills in Cameroon, through conservation action and education.

- Find out more about the work of the ACF by visiting www.africanconservation.org.

EASTERN LOWLAND GORILLA

'WHILE FACTIONS IN DR CONGO FIGHT FOR SUPREMACY AND
MINERAL RESOURCES, THE WORLD'S ONLY EASTERN LOWLAND
GORILLAS FIGHT FOR THEIR SURVIVAL'
THE GORILLA ORGANIZATION

Gorillas are one of our closest living relatives, and their normally placid, pensive disposition has rightly earned them the nickname of gentle giants. However, human actions have taken almost all populations of gorillas to the brink of extinction.

The Mountain Gorilla (*Gorilla beringei beringei*) has one of the smallest populations, but the encouraging news is that this has been increasing in recent years. Meanwhile, the neighbouring population of Eastern Lowland Gorillas has suffered an 80-90% decline since 2000 and we are all to blame in some way. The rapid growth of micro-technologies, from mobile phones to laptop computers, led to an enormous demand for the metal tantalum, used in capacitors. Deposits of tantalum, as well as tin, are found under the gorilla's habitat and opportunistic miners have degraded the environment and hunted the gorillas. Their habitat is also still under the control of rebel militias, and their survival hangs in the balance.

COMMON NAME: Eastern Lowland Gorilla (Grauer's Gorilla)

SCIENTIFIC NAME: *Gorilla beringei graueri*

SIZE: Males average 175cm in height, females 160cm.

STATUS: Endangered.

POPULATION: A census conducted in 1998 suggested there were approximately 17,000 Eastern Lowland Gorillas. Since then the population has been greatly reduced, and while it has not been possible to get a reliable estimate of the population size, at present it is thought that only around 2,000 to 3,000 gorillas survive.

LIFESPAN: Gorillas in the wild can live for between 30-35 years.

RANGE: The Eastern Lowland Gorilla is confined to the eastern provinces of the Democratic Republic of Congo.

THREATS: Hunting and degradation of their habitat.

the gorilla organization WHAT YOU CAN DO...

• Find out more about the issues and support the work of
  The Gorilla Organization at www.gorillas.org.

ETHIOPIAN WOLF

'ETHIOPIAN WOLVES PERCH ON THE EDGE OF SURVIVAL IN
EVER-SHRINKING MOUNTAIN HAVENS, PARADOXICAL VICTIMS OF
THEIR OWN EVOLUTIONARY SUCCESS AS MOUNTAIN SPECIALISTS'
CLAUDIO SILLERO, WildCRU

These elegant, long-legged wolves are found only in a handful of mountain
pockets in Ethiopia, living in family groups with a fascinating network
of social relationships and hierarchies. Because they are so specialised to
predate on high-altitude rodents, only 450 survive today in these highland
relicts, surrounded by expanding agriculture and threatened by disease
and persecution.

For over two decades the Ethiopian Wolf Conservation Programme
(EWCP) has been working to reduce the most urgent threats to their
survival. It monitors wolf packs, vaccinates domestic dogs – the reservoir
of deadly diseases – and raises awareness among children and local
communities of the plight of the wolves and the need to preserve the
mountains' natural resources needed by people sharing the land with
the wolves and those further down the slopes.

EWCP promotes these charismatic creatures as a flagship for the protection
of a rich array of endemic fauna and flora in the highlands of Ethiopia.

COMMON NAME: Ethiopian Wolf

SCIENTIFIC NAME: *Canis simensis*

STATUS : Endangered.

SIZE: 15-20kg, and 60cm at the shoulder, or about the size of an Alsatian dog.

POPULATION: 450 adults survive in six isolated mountain ranges, making them the rarest canid in the world, and Africa's most threatened carnivore. The largest population is found in the Bale Mountains National Park.

LIFESPAN: Up to 15 years in the wild. There are no Ethiopian Wolves in captivity.

RANGE: Found only in a handful of Ethiopia's mountains above 3,000m above sea level, with afroalpine heaths and grasslands where their rodent prey thrives.

THREATS: Rabies and canine distemper transmitted by the domestic dogs of mountain shepherds pose the most immediate threat. Ultimately, their survival depends on slowing down the loss of afroalpine habitat to subsistence agriculture and overgrazing.

WILDCRU
Wildlife Conservation Research Unit

WHAT YOU CAN DO...

- Find out more and donate to EWCP by visiting www.ethiopianwolf.org and www.wildcru.org;
  or email EWCP at ewcp@zoo.ox.ac.uk.

- You can also adopt an Ethiopian Wolf pack through the Born Free Foundation;
  visit www.bornfree.org.uk or call 01403 240170.

EURASIAN CURLEW

'CURLEWS ARE FAST DISAPPEARING; WE HAVE LOST MOST OF THE
IRISH POPULATION AND THERE ARE HUGE LOSSES IN WALES'
BRITISH TRUST FOR ORNITHOLOGY

It's now safe to say that the Eskimo Curlew is extinct and it is widely accepted that the Slender-billed Curlew has suffered the same fate. What is it about these large waders, with their downturned bills and evocative, bubbling calls that puts them at so much risk? Even the most widespread, our own Eurasian Curlew, is now causing concern, with worrying declines in numbers and loss of range.

In *Bird Atlas 2007-11*, involving 40,000 birdwatchers from across Britain and Ireland, we measured the changing fortunes: over 75% loss of range in Ireland in 40 years, and now also absent from much of western Wales, western Scotland and south-west England.

Many species are responding rapidly to the way that we are altering habitats and to changing weather patterns, including several moorland species. Some birds react positively, as we see with Little Egrets in wetlands, but others, such as the Eurasian Curlew, are losers.

COMMON NAME: Eurasian Curlew

SCIENTIFIC NAME:
Numenius arquata

SIZE: Up to 60cm in height with a wingspan of up to 100cm.

STATUS: Amber-listed species of conservation concern in the UK, Red-listed in Ireland and already classified as Near-threatened globally.

POPULATION: About 69,000 pairs in the UK.

LIFESPAN: Many of the problems may well be associated with poor breeding success. For those birds that do reach adulthood, the typical age attained is five years, with a maximum of over 32 years.

RANGE: Breeds across northern Europe and Asia from Ireland to eastern Russia.

THREATS: These are long-lived birds and lack of recruitment of enough juveniles to the population may have gone unnoticed for many years. As with seabird declines, it may take a while to appreciate the extent of the curlew's problems.

 **BTO** Looking out for birds

WHAT YOU CAN DO...

- *Bird Atlas 2007-11*, published by the British Trust for Ornithology (BTO), along with the Scottish Ornithologists' Club and BirdWatch Ireland, provides the evidence you need to speak knowledgeably about the changes to the bird fauna of Britain and Ireland. To read more about the book, visit www.bto.org/atlas.

- To get involved in other BTO surveys, visit www.bto.org.

- Support the work of the BTO by becoming a member. Email info@bto.org.

EURASIAN LYNX

'BY THE END OF THE 19TH CENTURY, IN MOST PARTS
OF EUROPE, THE LYNX HAD VANISHED FROM EXISTENCE'
PRO NATURA

One hardly ever sees the Eurasian Lynx – and not only because few survive.
This tuft-eared wildcat is quite shy, living in forests where it can hide itself
well, and is mostly active at dusk.

The lynx hunts small cloven-footed animals which it can sneak up on
masterfully. Its most important prey in Switzerland are deer and chamois.

By the end of the 19th century, in most parts of Europe, as in Switzerland,
the lynx had vanished from existence. Deforestation, a massive decrease of its
natural prey and hunting were to blame.

For a long time, Pro Natura has worked hard to bring back the lynx.
In 1971, the first lynx was reintroduced to Switzerland and Pro Natura
has vigorously supported the species ever since.

But once again, the 'alp tiger' must fight for pure survival in its
original habitat.

COMMON NAME: Eurasian Lynx

SCIENTIFIC NAME: *Lynx lynx*

SIZE: Up to 130cm in length with a
tail length of up to 25cm. Shoulder
height up to 70cm.

STATUS: Near-threatened.

POPULATION: Fewer than 50,000
(worldwide); approximately 150
in Switzerland.

LIFESPAN: The lynx reaches an
age of approximately 16 years.

RANGE: Found in the forests
of Europe and Asia (north of
the Himalayas).

THREATS: Destruction of its
habitat (deforestation), the decrease
of its natural prey, hunting and
a change in the natural dynamic
between species.

 WHAT YOU CAN DO...

- Become a member of the nature conservation organisation Pro Natura, or support its species
  protection effort by making a donation at www.pronatura.ch.

- Information about the Eurasian Lynx, and the specific needs for its environment, can be found at
  www.pronatura.ch and www.kora.ch.

EUROPEAN STAG BEETLE

'THE LOSS OF THE STAG BEETLE WOULD MEAN THE LOSS OF THE LARGEST AND MOST STRIKING LAND BEETLE IN BRITAIN. WE MUST ACT NOW TO CONSERVE THIS BEAUTIFUL INSECT'

PEOPLE'S TRUST FOR ENDANGERED SPECIES

With its shiny chestnut-brown wing cases (head and thorax are black) and huge antler-like jaws, the Stag Beetle is a top contender for Britain's most impressive invertebrate. They are almost prehistoric in appearance, and are particularly dramatic when in flight on still summer evenings.

Once common across western Europe, the Stag Beetle is becoming increasingly rare in many countries, and so it is vital that we work to conserve them in the UK, where more of them survive. The species depends on undisturbed decaying wood habitat. The female burrows down and lays her eggs near the rotting wood. These hatch into larvae, which feed on the supply of dead wood, taking up to seven years to grow before pupating into adults. In adult form, Stag Beetles usually live for a couple of months, searching for mates so that the cycle can continue. In addition to habitat loss, stag beetles fall victim to magpies and road traffic, and often drown in water butts.

COMMON NAME: European Stag Beetle

SCIENTIFIC NAME: *Lucanus cervus*

SIZE: Male up to 10cm in length, female up to 4.5cm.

STATUS: BAP (Biodiversity Action Plan) listed.

POPULATION: Population figures for the Stag Beetle are not known. They are in serious decline on mainland Europe, while here in the UK their range seems stable. However, isolation of populations through loss of habitat, particularly due to development, remains a threat.

LIFESPAN: Larvae take up to seven years to grow before pupating into adults. Their adult lives are short (four to eight weeks).

RANGE: South-east England and western Europe.

THREATS: Many are killed by magpies, or drowned in ponds and water butts. The larval form is very susceptible to predation, and loss of undisturbed habitat may be resulting in a shortage of egg-laying sites.

people's trust for endangered species | WHAT YOU CAN DO...

- Why not become a Stag Beetle-friendly gardener? Try creating a log pile in a quiet, shady area and avoid using insecticides in the garden.

- For more information on Stag Beetles, visit www.ptes.org. To take part in one of the People's Trust for Endangered Species' (PTES) national stag beetle monitoring surveys, go to www.greatstaghunt.org.

FLORIDA PANTHER

'FEWER THAN 150 PANTHERS ARE CONCENTRATED IN POCKETS OF LAND
IN SOUTH-WEST FLORIDA, WHERE THEY REMAIN THREATENED BY HUMAN
INTERFERENCE AND DEVELOPMENT'
SIERRA CLUB

The Florida Panther is the most endangered mammal in all of North America. It once freely roamed throughout the south-eastern United States, from Alabama to Tennessee to the Atlantic Ocean.

A subspecies of Puma (or Cougar), the habitat of this proud panther has been severely restricted by overdevelopment to just 5% of its historic range. Now, fewer than 150 panthers are concentrated in pockets of land in south-west Florida, where they remain threatened by human interference and development, with its remaining habitat threatened by climate disruption and sea level rise. Florida Panthers prefer hardwood hammocks and pinelands. The Saw Palmetto plant is the most important plant species, used by panthers for resting, stalking prey, and as dens.

Though it has been listed as Endangered since 1967, no critical habitat for this beautiful and rare cat has been designated. Meanwhile, dozens are killed each year by vehicle strikes. The Sierra Club and other organisations are fighting to ensure the Florida Panther's habitat remains wild so that this critical part of our nation's wild legacy can once again thrive.

COMMON NAME: Florida Panther

SCIENTIFIC NAME:
Felis concolor coryi

SIZE: Up to 240cm in length including tail. Shoulder height up to 80cm.

STATUS: Endangered.

POPULATION: Only 100-140 individuals of this endangered subspecies exist, confined to increasingly fragmented habitat in south Florida.

LIFESPAN: 12 years.

RANGE: South-west Florida.

THREATS: Fragmentation and destruction of habitat, intraspecific aggression and collisions with automobiles.

SIERRA CLUB
FOUNDED 1892

WHAT YOU CAN DO...

- Find out more about the work of the Sierra Club to conserve the Florida Panther by visiting www.sierraclub.org.

- The Sierra Club is involved in a wide range of projects to save lands and wildlife. To find out more, visit www.sierraclub.org.

FOSA

'THE FOSA IS SERIOUSLY UNDER THREAT FROM HUMAN ACTIVITIES SUCH AS HUNTING AND PERSECUTION, WHILE DEFORESTATION IS DESTROYING ITS NATURAL HABITAT'
DUKE UNIVERSITY, NORTH CAROLINA, USA

Sitting at the top of the food chain in Madagascar is the dynamic yet enigmatic Fosa, a relative of the civets. Reaching up to 80cm in body length, with a tail almost as long, it's the largest of Madagascar's carnivores. With cat-like claws and mongoose-like tenacity, this supreme killing machine lunches on lemurs, birds and reptiles, and helps keep its ecosystem in check.

Little is known about the Fosa itself, but we do know that it is seriously under threat from human activities such as hunting and persecution, while deforestation is destroying its natural habitat, resulting in a loss of biodiversity. In fact, less than 7% of its original habitat remains today.

In Madagascar's Ankarafantsika National Park, researchers from Duke University, North Carolina, are radio-tracking the movements and activity patterns of the ferocious Fosas, surveying the forest for prey populations and collecting radio-telemetry data. Since 2002, they've noted a significant decrease in the number of Fosa passing through their study areas – which may be attributed to the increasing numbers of feral dogs, and possibly wild cats, which bring threats to the Fosa, such as competition for resources, as well as rabies and other diseases.

The data collected by the scientists will help develop successful conservation plans for the species and its habitat, without compromising the wellbeing and livelihoods of local communities.

COMMON NAME: Fosa

SCIENTIFIC NAME: *Cryptoprocta ferox*

SIZE: Body 70-80cm in length, with a tail of 65-70cm.

STATUS: Vulnerable

POPULATION: Thought to be fewer than 2,500 individuals, and decreasing.

LIFESPAN: Around 15 years in the wild.

RANGE: Endemic to Madagascar.

THREATS: Habitat loss, hunting and persecution.

WHAT YOU CAN DO...

- Support Duke University's research work by joining an Earthwatch expedition to Madagascar's Ankarafantsika National Park, and help protect the fascinating Fosa and its fragile habitat.

- Find out how Friends of Madagascar is providing essential educational and health supplies to students in Madagascar at www.friendsofmadagascar.org

FRESHWATER PEARL MUSSEL

'THE FRESHWATER PEARL MUSSEL IS A FASCINATING SPECIES WHOSE
GLOBAL POPULATION HAS DECLINED BY OVER 90% IN THE LAST CENTURY'
FRESHWATER BIOLOGICAL ASSOCIATION

The Freshwater Pearl Mussel is a fascinating species whose global population has declined by over 90% in the last century. It has recently been reclassified as Critically Endangered (from Endangered) on the IUCN Red List of Threatened Species. The Freshwater Pearl Mussel has a complex life cycle that requires a salmonid fish host for its larval stage (known as glochidia) to grow and mature. It spends 9-11 months on the gills of its host before dropping into river gravels to continue its development. This parasitic stage is not thought to harm the host fish. Individuals become sexually mature between 12-15 years old and continue to reproduce until they die. Individuals can live to be over 130 years old.

The Freshwater Pearl Mussel inhabits very clean, nutrient- and calcium-poor rivers. Each adult can filter up to 50 litres of water per day and so helps to maintain water quality in its native rivers. Its drastic decline is due to a wide range of factors, including habitat degradation or destruction (through nutrient enrichment and aggravated sediment input), loss of host fish species and poaching. In England, a captive breeding programme was set up in 2007 by the Freshwater Biological Association (FBA), Environment Agency and Natural England to rear juvenile mussels for reintroduction into the wild. Along with other partners, the Environment Agency and Natural England are working to improve habitat conditions in the wild so that when juvenile mussels reared at the FBA are released, they stand a better chance of survival.

COMMON NAME:
Freshwater Pearl Mussel

SCIENTIFIC NAME:
Margaritifera margaritifera

SIZE: Up to 17cm in length.

STATUS: Critically Endangered (IUCN).

POPULATION: Several million individuals still present, but all populations are declining and some population numbers are critically low.

LIFESPAN: Long-lived; up to 60 years in the southern extent of its distributional range and over 130 years in the northern part of its range.

RANGE: Holarctic, in calcium- and nutrient-poor rivers and streams.

THREATS: Nutrient enrichment, aggravated sedimentation of habitat, habitat degradation, loss of fish hosts and poaching (only in some parts of its range).

WHAT YOU CAN DO...

- Support the Freshwater Pearl Mussel Ark Project at the FBA – the FBA runs a captive breeding programme for the Freshwater Pearl Mussel. To learn more about the species or the FBA, or to donate, visit www.fba.org.uk/freshwater-pearl-mussel-ark-project.

- Be a river champion – be vigilant for anyone disturbing habitat or individuals and, if you suspect poaching, get in touch with the local authority dealing with pearl mussel conservation.

GOULDIAN FINCH

'SAVING THE GOULDIAN FINCH REQUIRES URGENT, SWEEPING CHANGES TO LAND MANAGEMENT IN AUSTRALIA'S TROPICAL SAVANNAS'
AUSTRALIAN WILDLIFE CONSERVANCY

The multicoloured Gouldian Finch is endemic to the tropical savannas of northern Australia. Once found in dazzling flocks of thousands, in recent decades they have dwindled dramatically. The entire population now numbers fewer than 2,500 adult birds.

The reasons for this precipitous decline revolve around changes in land management during the last century. The introduction of large herbivores (cattle, horses, donkeys, buffalo) and a radical shift in fire patterns towards more extensive and frequent fires, have reduced seed production in the grass species that Gouldian Finches rely on for food. Many other bird species that eat grass seed have shown similar patterns of decline. Saving the Gouldian Finch and other threatened species of the tropical savannas requires a concerted effort by government and non-government conservation agencies and landowners (including pastoralists and Aboriginal communities) to manage fire and cattle across the vast landscapes of northern Australia.

COMMON NAME: Gouldian Finch

SCIENTIFIC NAME: *Erythrura gouldiae*

SIZE: 130-140 mm in length.

STATUS: Endangered.

POPULATION: Fewer than 2,500 adults.

LIFESPAN: Poor data, but probably one to two years in the wild, and up to four years in captivity.

RANGE: Previously across Australia's tropical savannas from Queensland, through the Northern Territory, to Western Australia. Reduced now to isolated populations, mainly in Western Australia and the Northern Territory, with only sporadic sightings of very small numbers of birds in Queensland.

THREATS: Changed fire patterns and grazing by cattle.

australian
wildlife
conservancy

WHAT YOU CAN DO...

- Support Australian Wildlife Conservancy (www.australianwildlife.org), a non-governmental organisation dedicated to saving Australia's threatened wildlife and ecosystems.

- Pay a visit to Mornington Wilderness Camp (www.australianwildlife.org/AWC-Sanctuaries/Mornington-Sanctuary/Mornington-Wilderness-Camp.aspx) to see Gouldian Finches in the wild, and to learn about Australian Wildlife Conservancy's work at Mornington and also at its other sanctuaries throughout Australia.

GRANDIDIER'S BAOBAB

'RECENT RESEARCH HAS SHOWN THAT OF THE THREE BAOBAB SPECIES IN THE MENABE REGION GRANDIDIER'S BAOBAB IS THE ONLY SPECIES USED EXTENSIVELY BY LOCAL PEOPLE'
GLOBAL TREES CAMPAIGN

Baobabs, with their distinctive upside-down shape, are one of the most charismatic group of trees in the world. Six out of the eight species of baobab are endemic to Madagascar, with three classified as Endangered and three as Near Threatened. Found on Madagascar's west coast, Grandidier's Baobab, locally known as the Renala, is an icon for both the Malagasy people and conservationists alike. These sacred trees are the home of ancestral spirits, their bark is traditionally used for medicine, rope-making and construction, and their nutritious fruits are used to make juice. They also have an important ecological role, providing flying foxes and some nocturnal lemurs with nectar and pollen.

Slash and burn agriculture, and over-exploitation of the tree's bark and fruit, have significantly reduced the population of mature trees and their natural regeneration, and now these conservation icons are gradually sliding towards extinction. Furthermore, the species has a very slow rate of regeneration, meaning that not enough new trees are replacing the older ones being lost.

Global Trees Campaign is supporting its partner Madagasikara Voakajy by supporting establishment of community-based organisations to help local people to actively protect the remaining mature trees that they revere. The project is also working with local schools to bolster natural populations through tree-planting initiatives; and regional education campaigns and competitions have been launched to help restore pride and raise attention to the plight of the country's national tree.

COMMON NAME: Grandidier's Baobab

SCIENTIFIC NAME: *Adansonia grandidieri*

SIZE: Up to 30m in height.

STATUS: Endangered.

POPULATION: Unknown.

LIFESPAN: Very long-lived – hundreds of years.

RANGE: Restricted to the south-west Madagascar, in the Menabe and Atsimo Andrefana regions.

THREATS: Fire and slash and burn agriculture; over-exploitation of bark.

GLOBAL TREES CAMPAIGN WHAT YOU CAN DO...

- 8,753 tree species – approximately 10% of the world's total – are listed as globally threatened. You can help save these by donating to www.globaltrees.org/support.htm

GREAT CRESTED NEWT

'GREAT CRESTED NEWTS ARE VULNERABLE TO RAPID DECLINE
DUE TO LOSS OF SUITABLE BREEDING PONDS'
FROGLIFE

Great Crested Newts are the most easily recognised species of newt in
Britain because of their size and colouring. Males exhibit a large crest
during the breeding season and the white flashes on the tail distinguish
them from the females. They have striking orange undersides with irregular
black markings, and each pattern is unique to that individual.

Great Crested Newts, although widespread throughout much of Britain,
are vulnerable to rapid loss and decline. The British population is among
the largest in Europe, where they are threatened in several countries. The
main threats to Great Crested Newts range from loss of suitable breeding
ponds, caused by water table reduction and ponds being filled in for site
development, to agrochemicals leaching into ponds and the stocking of newt
ponds with fish. Finally, terrestrial habitat destruction and fragmentation
complete the long list.

COMMON NAME:
Great Crested Newt

SCIENTIFIC NAME: *Triturus cristatus*

SIZE: Up to 17cm long.

STATUS: Least Concern.

POPULATION: The exact population
number is not known, but there
are believed to be around 100,000
occupied ponds in Britain.

LIFESPAN: Lives on average up to
14 years in the wild.

RANGE: Great Britain, western,
central and eastern Europe north of
the Alps up to central Scandinavia
and southern Finland. Usually found
below 1,100m.

THREATS: Deliberate filling in
or destruction of ponds; pond
loss through natural succession;
introduction of fish; chemical
pollution and nutrification of
breeding sites; loss of terrestrial
habitat; habitat fragmentation; poor
habitat management; and pond
deterioration through neglect.

froglife
leaping forward for
reptiles & amphibians

WHAT YOU CAN DO...

- Become a Froglife Friend (visit www.froglife.org). Donations contribute to various projects to help
  conserve native reptiles and amphibians.

- Help manage ponds and terrestrial habitat in a wildlife-friendly way. You can find out more ideas
  for this at www.froglife.org.

GREATER BAMBOO LEMUR

'THE IMMEDIATE CRISIS OF THE GREATER BAMBOO LEMUR HAS BEEN
AVERTED, BUT WITH ONLY 600 KNOWN IN THE WILD THEIR LONG-TERM
SURVIVAL IS STILL IN THE BALANCE'
THE ASPINALL FOUNDATION

Greater Bamboo Lemurs are one of the highest priority species in global mammal conservation. Considered critically endangered, they have no close living relatives, and only occur in a small number of bamboo thickets in and around the rainforests of eastern Madagascar. Their diet consists almost entirely of Madagascan giant bamboos. In the wet season they eat the cyanide-rich young bamboo ground shoots, while in the dry season they are the only lemur with jaws strong enough to rip open the tough bamboo stems. This highly specialised diet is probably the main reason for their very patchy distribution in the wild.

Discovering new populations in the wild was only possible with the help of local people who knew where to find high densities of bamboo, followed up by days of searching for the characteristic remains of bamboo devoured by the Greater Bamboo Lemurs. Once potential sites had been identified, immediate support of local communities to reduce threats to the sites and the lemurs was essential to ensure their survival. This strategy has recently led to Greater Bamboo Lemurs being removed from the list of the 25 most endangered primates in the world for the first time in a decade. However, the continued and long-term support of local communities is the only way to assure that this progress has not been in vain.

COMMON NAME: Greater Bamboo Lemur

SCIENTIFIC NAME: *Prolemur simus*

SIZE: Body up to 50cm in length. Tail up to 60cm.

STATUS: Critically Endangered.

POPULATION: Recent surveys and community-based conservation have increased the known wild population from 60 in 2007 to 600 in 2012.

LIFESPAN: Some Greater Bamboo Lemurs live for over 20 years.

RANGE: Greater Bamboo Lemurs occur in patches of giant bamboo in and near the rainforests of eastern Madagascar.

THREATS: Hunting is one threat to Greater Bamboo Lemurs, but can easily be stopped by community-based conservation projects. Habitat destruction due to slash-and-burn agriculture is more difficult to combat, while habitat fragmentation can lead to high extinction risk of small, isolated sub-populations.

WHAT YOU CAN DO...

- Support the community-based conservation work of The Aspinall Foundation in Madagascar, which protects more than half the total known population of Greater Bamboo Lemurs; visit www.aspinallfoundation.org/conservation.

- Madagascar is the only place in the world where lemurs exist in the wild, but of just over 100 known species, more than 90 are threatened with extinction. Raise awareness and funds among your local communities for lemur conservation in Madagascar – now is the time.

GREEK RED DAMSELFLY

'DRAGONFLIES AND DAMSELFLIES CURRENTLY FACE MORE THREATS TO THEIR HABITATS THAN AT ANY TIME IN THE PAST. WE NEED TO WORK NOW TO REDUCE THE THREATS TO THESE AMAZING INSECTS'
BRITISH DRAGONFLY SOCIETY

Dragonflies and damselflies are amazing insects with fascinating behaviour and majestic powers of flight. There are almost 6,000 known species of dragonfly and damselfly on the Earth today. The largest have a 19cm wingspan and the smallest a wingspan of less than 2cm. Around 325 million years ago, the ancestors of our dragonflies today had wingspans of up to 70cm!

Dragonflies belong to an order of insects known as the Odonata (meaning toothed jaws). This order includes the delicate damselflies or Zygoptera (meaning equal wings), as well as the larger and more powerful 'true' dragonflies or Anisoptera (meaning unequal wings).

In recent years, changes to the environment have threatened several species of dragonfly, including the Greek Red Damselfly. Land management has altered with increased use of pesticides and greater water abstraction. Ponds have been infilled and other waterbodies polluted. Development has encroached on our wild areas with more of the Earth becoming urbanised. Climate change is also threatening dragonflies, with more droughts and extreme weather conditions.

COMMON NAME: Greek Red Damselfly

SCIENTIFIC NAME: *Pyrrhosoma elisabethae*

STATUS: Endemic to Europe where it is Critically Endangered.

SIZE: Wing length 20-24mm; body length 36-38mm.

POPULATION: Small, declining populations. Kalkman and Lopau (2006) reported that the species had been seen on only 16 occasions.

LIFESPAN: The adults are on the wing from the end of April through until mid-June. The length of the complete life cycle is unknown, but it is likely to be two years, as its nearest relative, the Large Red Damselfly, has a two-year life cycle. It will spend the majority of its life underwater in its larval form.

RANGE: Balkan Peninsula, namely western Greece and southern Albania – it has been recorded from only eight locations.

THREATS: It is found on running water, including ditches, brooks and a slow-flowing river. None of its sites is protected and all are at risk.

British Dragonfly Society

WHAT YOU CAN DO...

- Dig a pond for dragonflies. Although garden ponds cannot compensate for the loss of natural habitats, they are nonetheless of considerable value for dragonflies.

- Send the British Dragonfly Society (BDS) records of your sightings of dragonflies so we can monitor how healthy the populations are.

- Find out more about the BDS by visiting www.british-dragonflies.org.uk and become a BDS member.

GREEN TURTLE

'HUMAN-RELATED CAUSES ARE THE TOP CONTRIBUTOR TO THE DRASTIC DECLINES IN GREEN SEA TURTLE POPULATIONS. WE MUST BECOME MORE AWARE OF OUR IMPACT ON THEIR EXISTENCE'
WIMARCS

Green Turtles are the largest of all the hard-shelled sea turtles, measuring over 100cm in carapace length and weighing on average 150kg. Named for the colour of their fat, adult Green Turtles are herbivores and feed near-shore on seagrasses and algae.

Since Green Turtles are often found close to shore, local harvesting, coastal development and pollution have a severe impact on this species. The high incidence of fibropapillomas, or cancer-like tumours, in coastal areas has led scientists to suspect that marine pollution may be involved in the development and transfer of this disease. Little is known about fibropapilloma, although it is believed that a virus causes the fatal, lobed tumours that may cover the skin, eyes and internal organs of this species. Its occurrence has reached epidemic proportions in many populations, severely threatening the health, vitality and future of this charismatic species. Comprehensive research, conservation and education efforts are needed to ensure the survival of Green Turtles.

COMMON NAME: Green Turtle

SCIENTIFIC NAME: *Chelonia mydas*

SIZE: Up to 1.5m in length.

STATUS: Endangered globally, with a continuing population decline.

POPULATION: Currently, it is estimated that approximately 88,000 adult female green turtles are nesting worldwide.

LIFESPAN: Unknown; the lifespan of the green turtle is estimated at up to 80 years.

RANGE: May be found in the warm waters of tropical and subtropical oceans worldwide.

THREATS: Fibropapilloma tumours, overexploitation for meat, shell and eggs, loss of nesting and foraging habitat due to coastal development, and incidental catch in fishing gear.

WHAT YOU CAN DO...

- Make a tax-deductible contribution to the West Indies Marine Animal Research and Conservation Service (WIMARCS) to support research into fibropapilloma, habitat utilisation and human impacts on foraging grounds. See www.wimarcs.org.

- Never pollute the ocean and always reduce your boat speed in coastal waters.

- Please don't drive vehicles or ride horses on a nesting beach. Don't allow dogs to dig on beaches during the nesting season. See www.wimarcs.org to decrease harmful light pollution.

GREY NURSE SHARK

'URGENT ACTION IS NEEDED TO PROPERLY PROTECT THIS SHARK'
AUSTRALIAN MARINE CONSERVATION SOCIETY

A short history of the Grey Nurse Shark paints a tale of mistaken identity and gross overfishing. Thousands of Grey Nurse Sharks were killed during the 1960s and 1970s along the east Australian coastline because of their ferocious appearance and undeserved reputation as a 'man eater'. The Grey Nurse Shark, however, is completely harmless and has become a favourite among divers who view these charismatic animals in their critical habitats.

Incidental and illegal fishing continues to deplete this species, and today it is estimated that fewer than 1,000 individuals remain along the east Australian coastline. Urgent action is needed to properly protect the Grey Nurse Shark and its habitat from all forms of fishing, particularly at the known critical habitat sites along the east Australian coastline.

Critical information is still unknown about where these sharks go during different stages of their life and research is under way in Australia to help identify other critical habitat for these endangered sharks.

COMMON NAME: Grey Nurse Shark

SCIENTIFIC NAME: *Carcharias taurus*

SIZE: Up to 3m long.

STATUS: Critically Endangered (Australian east coast population).

POPULATION: Fewer than 1,000 individuals probably remain on the east coast of Australia.

LIFESPAN: Aquaria: 16 years. Wild: unknown, but likely to live longer than aquarium species.

RANGE: Recorded all around Australia except for Tasmania, and in tropical and temperate waters of the Atlantic, Indian and western Pacific oceans.

THREATS: Incidental and illegal capture by recreational and commercial fishers, illegal shark finning and shark control programmes.

WHAT YOU CAN DO...

- Become an Australian Marine Conservation Society Sea Guardian and donate online to save our sharks at www.marineconservation.org.au or email amcs@amcs.org.au.

- Become an Ocean e-Activist to help save our sharks and other threatened marine wildlife. Visit www.marineconservation.org.au and make your voice heard today.

GURNEY'S PITTA

'ONE OF THE RAREST AND MOST BEAUTIFUL BIRDS OF SOUTH-EAST ASIA, FACING EXTINCTION DUE TO THE WHOLESALE DESTRUCTION OF ITS FOREST HABITAT'
BIRDLIFE INTERNATIONAL

Gurney's Pitta is a brilliantly coloured, but secretive bird of the forest floor – also sometimes called the 'jewel-thrush'. Only known from peninsula Thailand and adjacent southern Burma, it has a remarkable history. It was discovered in 1875, fairly widely collected and reported in the 1910s and 1920s, but last seen in 1936. Then, in 1986, a small population was rediscovered in southern Thailand, where around 20 pairs are now known to still exist.

In 2003, the ornithological world was stunned to hear of the discovery of a new, much larger population of this pitta in Burma. However, large areas of this species' habitat are in danger of being cleared. As a result, in 2005 the British Birdwatching Fair raised £200,000 towards helping to conserve Gurney's Pittas in South-east Asia. The bird epitomises many of the problems facing tropical rainforest species. Its greatest threats come from habitat destruction, with forest clearance for oil palm being a particular problem.

COMMON NAME: Gurney's Pitta
SCIENTIFIC NAME: *Pitta gurneyi*
SIZE: Average 20cm in length.
STATUS: Critically Endangered.
POPULATION: 10,000 to 17,200 mature individuals.
LIFESPAN: About five years.
RANGE: Occurs at one site in peninsula Thailand, and also in adjacent southern Tenasserim, Burma.
THREATS: The key reason for its decline has been the almost total clearance of lowland forest in peninsula Thailand through clear-felling for timber, unofficial logging and conversion to agriculture. By 1987, only 20-50km^2 of forest below 100m remained in peninsula Thailand, and this area continues to decline. Snare-line trapping for the cage-bird trade is also a serious threat.

BirdLife
INTERNATIONAL

WHAT YOU CAN DO...

- Visit the British Birdwatching Fair, held every summer at Britain's Rutland Water. Profits from the fair go towards conservation of species – such as the Gurney's Pitta – and habitats around the world.

- Find out more about the work of BirdLife International and its partners by visiting www.birdlife.org.

HAIRY-NOSED OTTER

'THE ILLEGAL WILDLIFE TRADE IS SEVERELY THREATENING THE FUTURE OF ALL FOUR SPECIES OF ASIAN OTTER, BUT ESPECIALLY THE RARE HAIRY-NOSED OTTER'
INTERNATIONAL OTTER SURVIVAL FUND

Throughout Asia, otters receive very little conservation attention as most effort is directed towards the larger, high-profile species. And yet otters are at the forefront of the wildlife trade, along with tigers and leopards. For every tiger skin found there are at least 10 otter skins, and one haul in Tibet had 778 otter skins. This included furs from the rare Hairy-nosed Otter.

In 1998, the Hairy-nosed Otter was believed to be extinct, but an IOSF-supported project in Thailand found small numbers. Since then a few isolated and highly threatened populations have been found in Cambodia, Vietnam and Indonesia.

In Indonesia there is a considerable trade in otters for pets. Most animals are wild-caught Asian Short-clawed Otters and the mother is killed in order to capture the cubs. Hairy-nosed Otters are also involved and in early 2013 four were found in Kalimantan. This species is particularly vulnerable and all four cubs died due to poor initial care.

Otters are excellent environmental indicators as they use both land and aquatic habitats. Both need to be in pristine condition for the otters to thrive.

In Asia, there are very few scientists working on otters and their habitats, and IOSF is training people to work within local communities, developing public awareness and education programmes.

Unless we work quickly to save the Hairy-nosed Otter, it will become extinct and this time there will be no miracle discovery.

COMMON NAME: Hairy-nosed Otter

SCIENTIFIC NAME: *Lutra sumatrana*

SIZE: 50-80cm in length with a tail 35-50cm in length.

STATUS: Endangered.

POPULATION: Unknown.

LIFESPAN: Unknown.

RANGE: Small isolated pockets in Thailand, Cambodia, Vietnam and Indonesia.

THREATS: The main threat is the illegal wildlife trade, as many otters are taken for fur and for pets. They are often regarded as pests by fishermen, who then kill them to supply the fur trade. Otters also suffer from wetland degradation and depleted food resources.

IOSF
INTERNATIONAL OTTER SURVIVAL FUND

WHAT YOU CAN DO...

• Make a donation or adopt an otter at www.ottershop.co.uk. You can also sign up for the monthly e-update and find out what the International Otter Survival Fund is doing to help hairy-nosed otters and the other 12 species of otter worldwide at www.otter.org.

• Report to IOSF any incidents of trade in otters – furs, pet markets – or if you see them being used in a circus.

HAWAIIAN COTTON TREE

'WITH NEW PLANTS AVAILABLE AND CAREFUL CROSSING, THERE
IS HOPE FOR RESTORING THIS BEAUTIFUL SPECIES TO THE WILD'
CENTER FOR PLANT CONSERVATION

Native plants are key to maintaining life on Earth. Through pervasive habitat loss and invasive species, however, many native plant species are now imperiled. *Kokia cookei*, also known as the Hawaiian Cotton Tree, is one of the rarest plant species in the world. It's one of more than 750 imperiled US species with seeds or cuttings secure in the Center for Plant Conservation's National Collection of Endangered Plants, cared for by 39 botanical institutions.

The last known wild plants disappeared in the early 1900s, after its natural forest environment had been steadily replaced over centuries by shrubland and introduced plants, although a single seed-grown plant survived in cultivation until 1978. After the death of the last whole individual, Waimea Valley continued propagating a few clonal plants through grafting, but seeds from these plants usually were weak and short-lived. After many years of work, scientists at Lyon Arboretum are producing whole plants on their own rootstock, using tissue culture techniques with seed embryos. With new plants available and careful crossing, there is hope for restoring this beautiful species to the wild.

COMMON NAME:
Hawaiian Cotton Tree

SCIENTIFIC NAME: *Kokia cookei*

SIZE: 4-5m high.

STATUS: Extinct in the wild.

DESCRIPTION: This deciduous tree, closely related to cotton, sports lobed leaves and boasts stunning red undulating flowers.

POPULATION: About 23 plants in cultivation in five different locations.

RANGE: The species occurred in the Hawaiian islands in the dryland forests on Molokai, a habitat mostly destroyed.

THREATS: Exotic, invasive plants, heavy grazing, habitat conversion to agriculture, lack of naturally rooted plants and lack of viable seed production.

WHAT YOU CAN DO...

- Join the Center for Plant Conservation's (CPC) Friends programme to support work assisting 39 botanic gardens with conservation programmes. Speak to your local or national lawmakers about the need to support plant conservation. Volunteer at your local botanic garden.

- Find out more about CPC's work in Hawaii and the rest of the US by visiting its website at www.centerforplantconservation.org.

HUMPHEAD WRASSE

'INTENSIVE AND SELECTIVE FISHING FOR THE LIVE FOOD TRADE
MEANS THAT POPULATIONS ARE DECLINING AROUND THE WORLD'
CORAL CAY CONSERVATION

Coral reefs are home to thousands of species worldwide, supporting around 25% of all known marine species, while covering only 0.5% of the sea floor. They are complex systems: the living corals not only providing food and shelter for other organisms, but dynamically interacting and responding to them. Over millions of years of evolution, a delicate balance has been developed between the complex web of living organisms and their non-living environment. This balance can be irrevocably disrupted by seemingly small changes in conditions, as we have seen worldwide with mass coral bleaching occurring as a result of temperature rises of just a few degrees Celsius.

By selectively removing certain species because they are good to eat or attractive to the aquarium industry, we are affecting the relationships between predators and their prey, disrupting food webs and ultimately impacting on the organisms that create the reef itself: the corals.

The Humphead Wrasse is just one species that has been affected by overfishing on a global scale. A large fish, which can reach sizes of over 2m in length, individuals grow slowly and don't reach sexual maturity until they are eight years old. Intensive and selective fishing of this species, primarily for the live food trade, means that populations are declining around the world.

COMMON NAME: Humphead Wrasse, Maori Wrasse or Napoleon Wrasse

SCIENTIFIC NAME: *Cheiliuns undulatus*

SIZE: Males up to 2m in length. Females up to 1m.

STATUS: Endangered.

POPULATION: Unknown globally, though considered uncommon and decreasing.

LIFESPAN: Over 30 years.

RANGE: Widespread throughout the tropical Indo-Pacific.

THREATS: Overfishing and habitat loss.

WHAT YOU CAN DO...

- Sign up to a Coral Cay Conservation expedition and contribute to one of our ongoing conservation projects around the world. Go to www.coralcay.org for more information.

- Respect the marine environment and the resources that come from it. Try to find out if the fish you are eating has been caught sustainably and avoid eating endangered species such as the Humphead Wrasse.

IRISH HARE

'THE IRISH HARE HAS BEEN OF MAJOR CONSERVATION CONCERN SINCE THE 1980s FOLLOWING A POPULATION DECLINE THAT WAS LARGELY A RESULT OF CHANGES IN LAND MANAGEMENT'
ULSTER WILDLIFE

The Irish Hare is a sub-species of mountain hare and is the only lagomorph native to Ireland. Irish Hares require a variety of different habitats: during the day they seek shelter in rushes and hedgerows, whereas at night, they require improved grassland that offers good-quality grazing.

The Irish Hare has been of major conservation concern since the 1980s following a population decline that was largely a result of changes in land management, namely agricultural intensification and landscape homogenisation. Introduction of the non-native Brown Hare to Ireland during the late 19th century has also posed a significant threat. Breeding surveys carried out during 2005 in Mid-Ulster and West Tyrone showed that Brown Hares now comprise more than half the hare population. In areas where the two species are occurring, there is evidence to suggest that not only are Brown Hares taking over from Irish Hares in lowland areas, there is also the added danger of hybridisation where both species co-exist.

With help from trained volunteers, Ulster Wildlife are leading Irish Hare Conservation work in Northern Ireland – surveying and monitoring populations across the country, and are working with landowners to ensure that there is ample habitat diversity.

COMMON NAME: Irish Hare

IRISH NAME: An Giorria (girr-ee-ah)

SCIENTIFIC NAME: *Lepus timidus hibernicus*

SIZE: Up to 50cm in length.

STATUS: All-Ireland priority species as a result of substantial decline over the past 15-25 years.

POPULATION: The population undergoes cyclical fluctuations but in 2010, during a period widely believed to be at the crest of an Irish Hare population fluctuation, there was an estimated 41,000 Irish Hares in Northern Ireland.

LIFESPAN: Maximum lifespan of nine years.

RANGE: Only found throughout Ireland.

THREATS: Habitat loss, invasive species and mortality of leverets from silage cutting.

Ulster Wildlife WHAT YOU CAN DO…

- Help to survey Irish Hares. Despite the recent doubling of the Irish Hare population, numbers still remain low and vulnerable. We need to monitor existing populations to establish where and what issues threaten their survival.

- If you know any farmers or land-owners, encourage them to maintain mixed habitat in their landscape. It is important to allow rush cover to develop in harder-to-reach sections of fields. Tall, thick hedgerows also provide excellent shelter, not just for Irish Hares, but for livestock and wildlife in general.

JAVAN LEAF MONKEY

'THIS ENDEMIC INDONESIAN PRIMATE IS
THREATENED BY HUNTING AND POACHING'
PROFAUNA INDONESIA

At least 2,500 Javan Leaf Monkeys are hunted every year, for both the pet trade and the meat trade, particularly at Saradan-Ngawi in east Java. In addition, the species is often sold as a pet on the side of the road, painted by the vendors in garish colours to draw attention to it. There are several large bird markets all over the island of Java, in which this monkey can be found for sale.

Meanwhile, in Banyuwangi, East Java, this monkey is frequently eaten at parties, where it is prized as an accompaniment to alcohol, and in some quarters even believed to be a cure for asphyxia – and all this despite the fact that the Javan Leaf Monkey is a protected primate.

ProFauna encourages the government to provide assistance on the confiscation operation of the illegally traded Javan Leaf Monkeys, which are also known as Javan Langurs. In increasing public awareness, ProFauna's activists wear Javan Langur-like costumes to educate the children about the primate's conservation.

COMMON NAME: Javan Leaf Monkey or Javan Langur

SCIENTIFIC NAME: *Trachypitecus auratus*

SIZE: Around 55cm in length with a 98cm tail.

STATUS: Protected by law in Indonesia, CITES Apendix II.

POPULATION: Unknown. At least 2,500 are illegally hunted every year.

LIFESPAN: Up to 12 years in captivity: its lifespan in the wild has not yet been determined.

RANGE: The Indonesian islands of Java, Bali and Lombok.

THREATS: Hunting and trading, for both the meat and pet trades.

ProFauna INDONESIA WHAT YOU CAN DO...

- Find out more about ProFauna's Indonesian campaign to stop Javan Leaf Monkey trade by visiting www.profauna.net.

- Visit the same website to discover how you can help ProFauna International save a wide range of threatened Indonesian wildlife.

JOCOTOCO ANTPITTA

'THE TOTAL WORLD POPULATION OF THIS NEWLY
DISCOVERED SPECIES IS PROBABLY ONLY A FEW HUNDRED'
FUNDACIÓN JOCOTOCO

The Jocotoco Antpitta can be considered emblematic of the hundreds of
endemic and threatened animals, and thousands of such plant species which
are found in the tropical Andes. It was discovered in the cloud forest of
the Amazon basin in Ecuador in November 1997, and in January 1998,
Fundación Jocotoco (FJ) was established, with a mission to protect this
amazing bird in its habitat.

The known population is only about 50 birds, of which 75% are now
protected inside the foundation's Cerro Tapichalaca reserve. The total
world population is probably only about a few hundred, and its habitat
is fragmented and depleted by deforestation, burning during dry spells
and cattle farming.

FJ had 11 reserves by 2012, providing protected habitat for nearly 50
threatened bird species, many large mammals (including Spectacled Bear,
Mountain Tapir and Jaguar), dozens of threatened Andean frogs and
hundreds of endemic/threatened plants.

COMMON NAME: Jocotoco Antpitta
('Jocotoco' is the local name
describing the bird's call)

SCIENTIFIC NAME: *Grallaria ridgelyi*

SIZE: 22cm in length.

STATUS: Endangered.

POPULATION: Only 50 known
individuals; likely estimated world
total: a few hundred.

LIFESPAN: Not known – probably
about 10 years.

RANGE: Very small range, found
in a 2,300 to 2,700m altitude
band (about 1-2km wide) in wet
cloud forest along about 50km
of Andean east-slope in the far
south of Ecuador, Rio Chinchipe,
to the border with Peru.

THREATS: Habitat loss and serious
fragmentation through forest
clearance, burning and cattle farming.

WHAT YOU CAN DO...

- Support Fundación Jocotoco's programme to protect threatened species in the Andes, which it does
  by increasing the size of the reserves, or by helping fund the long-term management of them by
  employing local people.

- Visit the website www.fjocotoco.org or see the World Land Trust website, www.worldlandtrust.org.

KIPUNJI

'AFRICA'S RAREST MONKEY REMAINS SERIOUSLY THREATENED'
SOUTHERN HIGHLANDS CONSERVATION PROGRAMME

Discovered by scientists from the Wildlife Conservation Society's Southern Highlands Conservation Programme in 2003, the Kipunji was first thought to be one of the mangabeys, a wide-spread family of African monkeys. However, genetic and skeletal analysis in 2006 showed the animal belonged to an entirely new genus (*Rungwecebus*), the first new genus of African monkey for more than 80 years. That such a discovery could be made in east Africa, where wildlife was assumed to be well known, astonished biologists and further demonstrated the considerable biological value of Tanzania's neglected Southern Highlands.

Unsurprisingly, the Kipunji is Africa's rarest monkey and is seriously threatened by hunting, illegal logging and habitat change, especially on Mount Rungwe, which holds the largest population. Forest destruction not only reduces the monkey's habitat but also forces it out of the forest to raid crops and be hunted in the process.

COMMON NAME: Kipunji

SCIENTIFIC NAME: *Rungwecebus kipunji*

SIZE: 85-90cm in height.

STATUS: Critically Endangered.

POPULATION: A complete census has shown that only 1,000 individuals exist.

LIFESPAN: As it is so new to science, the Kipunji's lifespan is not yet known.

DIET: The Kipunji is omnivorous, but favours fruit. It has at least 122 known food plants.

RANGE: The Kipunji only occurs in montane forest in south-west Tanzania at altitudes between 1,300 and 2,450m in about 70km^2 of Rungwe-Livingstone and about 6km^2 of Ndundulu forests.

THREATS: Logging, charcoal-making, poaching and unmanaged resource extraction are common. Widely hunted by humans as retribution for, and prevention against, the raiding of crops.

WHAT YOU CAN DO...

- Support the Kipunji Fund by contacting kipunji@gmail.com or wcstanzania@wcs.org.

- Visit www.wcstanzania.org or www.wcs.org to find out more about the work of the Southern Highlands Conservation Programme on the Kipunji and other wildlife.

LEATHERBACK TURTLE

'MARINE TURTLES HAVE SWUM OUR OCEANS FOR AT LEAST 110 MILLION YEARS,
BUT IN JUST THE LAST 100 YEARS, MANKIND HAS THREATENED THEIR EXISTENCE'
MARINE CONSERVATION SOCIETY

Unlike other reptiles, Leatherback Turtles generate their own body heat and are insulated by a thick layer of fat. This allows them to dive to depths of more than 1,000m and migrate thousands of kilometres across the ocean from their tropical nesting beaches to cooler seas in search of their favourite jellyfish prey.

These incredible migrations are hazardous and thousands of Leatherbacks entangle and drown in fishing nets set inshore in the tropics, get snagged on swordfish and tuna longlines set on the high seas, and occasionally get caught in the buoy ropes of crab and lobster pots set in temperate waters. They also eat floating marine litter, such as plastic bags and balloons, probably mistaking them for jellyfish. Once ingested, plastic can block a turtle's gut and lead to death by starvation.

These and other threats mean that without our help the critically endangered Leatherback faces an uncertain future in much of its range.

COMMON NAME: Leatherback Turtle

SCIENTIFIC NAME: *Dermochelys coriacea*

SIZE: Approx 2m kong.

STATUS: Critically Endangered.

POPULATION: There may be approximately 40,000 to 80,000 adult female leatherbacks nesting on beaches around the world, according to latest estimates.

LIFESPAN: Unknown but, like the closely related terrestrial tortoises, the leatherback's life may span many decades.

RANGE: The most widespread reptile on Earth and occurs in all ocean basins and the Mediterranean Sea.

THREATS: Climate change, interaction with coastal and high-seas fishing gear, egg harvesting, nesting beach development, marine litter and over-exploitation for meat.

WHAT YOU CAN DO...

- Turtles can die after swallowing marine litter, so make sure yours doesn't get in the sea. The Marine Conservation Society (MCS) aims to protect our seas, shores and wildlife and campaigns for litter-free seas. To find out more, visit www.mcsuk.org.

- Adopt-a-Turtle with MCS and help the conservation projects that MCS supports. Contact MCS or visit www.mcsuk.org.

LION

'KNOWN AS THE KING OF THE BEASTS, LIONS HAVE ALWAYS BEEN THE ULTIMATE PRIZE, WHETHER IT BE FOR A STUNNING PHOTOGRAPH OR, TRAGICALLY, FOR A HUNTER'S TROPHY WALL. BUT THEIR TIME IS RUNNING OUT'
CARE FOR THE WILD

While an accurate population tally is difficult, by most accounts Lion numbers have plummeted over the past three decades. Some 25 African countries have declared that their Lion populations have gone, while even in traditional 'strongholds', numbers are dwindling.

The dangers to Lions are numerous. Habitat loss affects populations and leads to human-wildlife conflict, resulting in deaths to both man and beast. Close contact can also lead to disease spreading through Lion populations with shattering effect.

Lion meat is served as an exotic dish, while Lion bones and other body parts are desired by users of traditional Chinese medicine – a huge and growing market that could devastate remaining Lion populations within a matter of decades.

Trophy hunting, massive in the 1970s, continues to be a problem. In South Africa, the business is so lucrative that more Lions are now bred in captivity than survive in the wild. These Lions are first used to attract unsuspecting tourists wanting a photo with a cute cub, and then released into confined areas to be shot at close range for trophies.

Ultimately, the international community needs to wake up to the problem before it is too late.

COMMON NAME: Lion

SCIENTIFIC NAME: *Panthera leo*

SIZE: Average 1.95m in length with an average tail length of 84cm. Shoulder height up to 90cm.

STATUS: Extinct in many countries; Endangered in India; Vulnerable in Africa.

POPULATION: Populations are hard to estimate, but it is suggested that the number in Africa has gone from around 200,000 to 300,000 in the 1970s to about 15,000 to 25,000 now.

LIFESPAN: 10-14 years in the wild; 20 years in captivity.

RANGE: Sub-Saharan Africa, with a small population remaining in India. Until the late Pleistocene, around 10,000 years ago, Lions ranged across Africa; from western Europe to India, and from Canada down to Peru.

THREATS: Trophy hunting, habitat loss, human-wildlife conflict, bushmeat and using body parts for commercial sale have all played their part.

WHAT YOU CAN DO...

- Support Care for the Wild's various international projects which Rescue, Protect and Defend wildlife across the world, and raise awareness on issues such as the plight of the lions. Visit www.careforthewild.com for more information.

- As a tourist, do not encourage the cruelty or abuse of animals. Find out how to be an animal-friendly tourist at www.right-tourism.org.

LITTLE WHIRLPOOL RAM'S-HORN SNAIL

'GLOBAL WARMING PROBABLY POSES THE GREATEST SINGLE LONG-TERM THREAT TO THIS AND MANY OTHER RARE SPECIES'
CONCHOLOGICAL SOCIETY OF GREAT BRITAIN & IRELAND

The Little Whirlpool Ram's-Horn Snail is a rare and vulnerable mollusc, confined to an equally scarce and endangered habitat, that of floodplain and coastal grazing marsh. These are typically flat expanses adjacent to the slow-flowing lower reaches of rivers where farmers have traditionally grazed animals and cut meadows for hay. Grazing marshes are typically bisected by networks of freshwater drains, and this species lives in the clean waters of only a few of the most pristine channels, always in association with a rich diversity of other freshwater animals and plants.

This snail is at risk from many factors. The conversion of traditionally managed areas to arable crops and intensive grass production typically lowers ditch water levels and adds fertiliser run-off. This 'junk-food' for plants creates 'over-enriched' waters that kill the snail together with other freshwater animals and plants. A final and increasing danger is global warming. Sea-level rise threatens all *Anisus* sites with saltwater intrusion.

Good news came in 2011, when the Government announced that three areas would become candidate Special Areas of Conservation (cSAC) for the snail. These are the Arun Valley cSAC (including Amberley Wild Brooks and Pulborough Brooks), Pevensey Levels cSAC and the snail was added to the existing Broads SAC, which lies mostly in Norfolk.

COMMON NAME: Little Whirlpool Ram's-Horn Snail

SCIENTIFIC NAME: *Anisus vorticulus*

SIZE: 5mm.

STATUS: UK BAP Priority Species, and also appears on two European Union 'Habitats Directive' annexes, II and IV.

POPULATION: In the UK only known from a few ditches in the Norfolk Broads / East Suffolk, Pevensey Levels Levels and Arun Valley in West Sussex, where it is declining. Populations have been lost from Lewes in Sussex and Staines in Surrey within the past 30 years. It is also Critically Endangered in Germany and the Czech Republic.

LIFESPAN: The snail has an annual life cycle.

RANGE: Occurs very locally throughout central and southern Europe.

THREATS: Agricultural fertilisers and changes of land use from traditional grazing to intensive agricultural practices; removal of grazing cattle; over-frequent dredging. An increasing threat is from sea-level rise leading to the saltwater flooding of ditches.

WHAT YOU CAN DO...

- Support sustainable national, local and personal lifestyle policies that minimise greenhouse emissions. Global warming probably poses the greatest single threat to this snail and many other rare species that are living in habitats only found in lowland areas close to sea level.

- Find out more about the conservation work of the Conchological Society of Great Britain & Ireland by visiting www.conchsoc.org.

LONG-EARED OWL

'GREATER AWARENESS OF THIS OWL IS NEEDED TO ENSURE ITS CONSERVATION'
HAWK AND OWL TRUST

If there was a prize for the least-known bird in Britain, the Long-eared Owl would be the winner. This secretive, nocturnal bird, with its cryptic plumage, is extraordinarily good at hiding and even its call is soft and easily missed.

Competition with its arch-rival, the Tawny Owl, could be one of the limiting factors. It is the commonest owl in Ireland, where there are no Tawny Owls.

The Long-eared Owl is a bird of the forest edge and small copses, and in some places it even nests in small hawthorns in hedgerows. Massive hedge removal in the second half of the 20th century and loss of lowland heathland – one of its favoured hunting grounds – to housing and other developments have diminished the population.

Artificial wicker baskets, if there is a scarcity of natural nest sites, have been successful where there are suitable feeding areas. Greater awareness of this owl is needed to ensure its conservation.

COMMON NAME: Long-eared Owl

SCIENTIFIC NAME: *Asio otus*

SIZE: Length 33-37cm; wingspan 90-100cm.

STATUS: Protected under the EU Birds Directive

POPULATION: Some 1,460 to 4,770 breeding pairs in England, Scotland and Wales, with a similar number in Ireland. European status: 205,000 (2% in Britain and Ireland).

LIFESPAN: 52% mortality in first year; oldest wild owl is a Long-eared at more than 27 years.

RANGE: Resident in much of Europe, northern Asia and North America.

THREATS: Loss of habitat and lack of knowledge, as often overlooked.

WHAT YOU CAN DO...

- Visit www.hawkandowl.org or contact Hawk and Owl Trust at PO Box 400, Bishops Lydeard, Taunton TA4 3WH, phone 0844 984 2824 or e-mail enquiries@hawkandowl.org.

- Adopt a Box (website as above). The money raised helps the trust with its conservation projects, including Long-eared Owls.

MANGROVE FINCH

'THE RAREST OF DARWIN'S FINCHES IS ANOTHER
REMINDER OF THE FRAGILITY OF THE GALAPAGOS ISLANDS'
CHARLES DARWIN FOUNDATION

The Mangrove Finch occurs only in the mangrove forests of the western Galapagos Islands (Isabela and Fernandina). Now confined to just two patches of mangrove in a combined area of 30ha and with an estimated population of approximately 100 individuals, it currently is one of the most range-restricted species in the world and the most endangered bird in the archipelago.

Mangrove Finches are threatened mainly during their nesting stage by two introduced species: Black Rats (*Rattus rattus*), which predate on eggs and chicks, and a parasitic fly (*Philornis downsi*), which at its larval stage parasitises chicks, causing a very high mortality.

At present, rat populations are under control and fledgling success has increased. Unfortunately, no control methods exist for the fly. Furthermore, protecting the nests is quite challenging since they are typically found high up in the canopy (up to 20m high).

Developing control techniques for *Philornis* is of highest priority and one of the hardest challenges that our scientists and Galapagos National Park Directorate are now dealing with. This is being done through strategic research plans and concerted international action. At stake is the first bird extinction ever to occur in the Galapagos Islands.

COMMON NAME: Mangrove Finch

SCIENTIFIC NAME: *Camarhynchus heliobates*

SIZE: 140mm in length

STATUS: Critically Endangered; extremely high risk of extinction in the wild.

SIZE: Weighs between 18-22g, wing measurement around 71mm.

POPULATION: Estimated to be 100 individuals.

LIFESPAN: Unknown, some banded individuals over seven years old.

RANGE: Fernandina (now extinct) and Isabela Islands.

THREATS: Predation by introduced rats and a parasitic fly; plus severe range restriction.

fundación
Charles Darwin
foundation
WHAT YOU CAN DO...

- Your commitment and support will help secure a sustainable future for Galapagos ecosystems and its unique species.

- For details on how you can support our work visit: www.darwinfoundation.org.

- For the latest project updates visit our Facebook page: www.facebook.com/darwinfoundation.

MARSH FRITILLARY

'BUTTERFLIES ARE AMONG THE MOST BEAUTIFUL AND FASCINATING CREATURES ON THE PLANET, BUT THEIR NUMBERS ARE DWINDLING RAPIDLY AS BREEDING HABITATS ARE DESTROYED'
BUTTERFLY CONSERVATION

Butterflies represent both the beauty and fragility of nature, but it's a sad fact that they are declining faster than most other groups of wildlife. They are very sensitive to change and are valuable indicators of the health of the environment: where butterflies thrive, nature is in balance.

The Marsh Fritillary epitomises the threats facing butterflies. Its caterpillars feed on just one main food plant, Devil's-bit Scabious, which grows in unfertilised, flower-rich pastures. Suitable habitats are maintained by low-intensity, traditional grazing, usually by cattle.

However, such habitats have been lost at a staggering rate across Europe as pastures are converted to arable land, drained or 'improved' with artificial fertiliser. In the UK it is now restricted to the west coast of Scotland, western Wales, Northern Ireland and the south-west and parts of central southern England. In the UK, over 92% of such pastures were lost during the 20th century, leaving remaining patches small and isolated. Butterfly Conservation is working to restore more suitable habitats.

COMMON NAME: Marsh Fritillary

SCIENTIFIC NAME: *Euphydryas aurinia*

SIZE: Wingspan up to 50mm.

STATUS: Vulnerable, owing to rapid decline across Europe.

POPULATION: Exact European population not known, but around 400 colonies are estimated to survive in the UK. Populations are renowned for their large fluctuations, which make them especially prone to local extinction. They therefore need extensive areas of breeding habitat to survive.

LIFESPAN: A single generation per year, with adults living just 5-10 days.

RANGE: Found across Europe.

THREATS: Continued habitat destruction and lack of suitable management. Habitat fragmentation is a growing threat.

Butterfly Conservation
Saving butterflies, moths and their habitats

WHAT YOU CAN DO...

- Join Butterfly Conservation and support its work to save butterflies and moths in the UK and across Europe. You can also contribute to its world-leading recording and monitoring schemes.

- Find out more about its work and join online at www.butterfly-conservation.org.

MEDITERRANEAN MONK SEAL

'THIS IS ONE OF THE RAREST MAMMALS IN THE WORLD,
AND THE MOST ENDANGERED MARINE MAMMAL IN EUROPE'
EURONATUR

Mediterranean Monk Seals were once widespread all over the Mediterranean, the Black Sea and the adjacent Atlantic coast. Nowadays, the remaining population is estimated to comprise only 350 to 450 individuals, which are highly dispersed into small groups, frequently consisting of only five to seven animals. The total population size of these rare marine mammals has been constantly declining in the past. Having been hunted for centuries, Monk Seals have left the beaches and withdrawn into caves and inaccessible creeks to reproduce and raise their pups. Yet ever-expanding tourist activities intrude on the habitats of these shy animals and industrial fisheries cause high disturbance. Additionally, the over-exploitation of fish has resulted in a shortage of the Monk Seal's diet. Moreover, these rare marine mammals continue to be drowned in fisher nets, becoming entangled when preying on the caught fish. In order to save this species, there is an urgent need to establish, maintain and guard protected areas in which the Monk Seals can reproduce without human disturbance and intervention.

In recent years, intense protection efforts made to support the subpopulation of Cabo Blanco in Mauritania showed that strict protection of the Monk Seal habitats supports the stabilisation of the species. Other important measures are environmental education and support for coastal fishermen in finding alternative income and fishing methods.

COMMON NAME: Mediterranean Monk Seal

SCIENTIFIC NAME: *Monachus monachus*

SIZE: Average length 2.4m.

STATUS: Critically Endangered.

POPULATION: The most endangered pinniped species in the world, with an estimated total population of 350-450 individuals in 2008.

LIFESPAN: Mediterranean Monk Seals can live up to 30 years or more.

RANGE: Widespread, but highly fragmented. In the Mediterranean, the most important breeding sites are on islands in the Ionian and Aegean Seas, and along the coasts of Greece and western Turkey. The two surviving colonies in the Atlantic are at Cabo Blanco in northern Mauritania and a smaller subpopulation at the Desertas Islands in the Madeira Islands group.

THREATS: Loss of habitat, overfishing, entanglement in fishing nets and direct persecution by fishermen, disturbance at breeding places and chemical pollution.

euronatur WHAT YOU CAN DO...

- Support one of the local projects coordinated in conjunction with EuroNatur (www.euronatur.org) in order to protect the remaining Mediterranean Monk Seal populations and improve the situation of this Critically Endangered species.

- Get informed about the threats to marine mammals and how you can help by visiting OceanCare at www.oceancare.org. With your support it can continue to apply its experience in protection of marine mammals and the oceans.

NATTERJACK TOAD

'DURING THE 20TH CENTURY THIS SPECIALIST AMPHIBIAN WAS LOST FROM MORE THAN 75% OF ITS KNOWN LOCATIONS IN BRITAIN'
THE AMPHIBIAN AND REPTILE CONSERVATION TRUST

Natterjack Toads live in open habitats, such as sand dunes, heathland and the upper reaches of salt marshes, where there is plenty of open ground and short vegetation. These areas were historically kept open by natural processes and through grazing and small scale digging for minerals. Natterjacks are highly adapted to these environments; with their short legs they actively hunt invertebrate prey, which gives the species its colloquial name of the Running Toad. They are able to avoid extremes of temperature and drying out by burrowing.

Natterjacks breed in shallow, often temporary (ephemeral) ponds where, attracted by the loud churring call of the males, females will lay strings of spawn, each with several thousand eggs.

During the 20th century more than 75% of the known colonies in Britain for this specialist amphibian were lost – some because of intensified agriculture, forestry or development, but many simply became unsuitable because of changes in the way that the land was managed. Fortunately, the Natterjack colonies have a great capacity to recover once key habitat features have been restored. The management work might be as straightforward as recreating breeding ponds or increasing the number of stock grazing the site, but this work and the on-going maintenance requires funding.

COMMON NAME: Natterjack Toad

SCIENTIFIC NAME: *Bufo calamita*

SIZE: Average length 6-8cm.

STATUS: Vulnerable at the edges of its range, but locally abundant and not endangered in the core.

POPULATION: In Britain there is a total of about 50 colonies.

LIFESPAN: In the wild males can live to about eight or nine years, and females, because of their lower risk of predation, can live to 12-15 years.

RANGE: The world range of this species is western Europe from Spain and Portugal through central and northern Europe to the Baltic States of the former USSR, Britain, Republic of Ireland and Sweden.

THREATS: At sites where the habitat has not been used for housing, agriculture or forestry, the main threats are the loss of breeding ponds and changes in the terrestrial habitat to favour more common frogs and toads.

amphibian and reptile conservation WHAT YOU CAN DO...

- Find out more about the work of The Amphibian and Reptile Conservation Trust and, if you live in Britain, whether Natterjacks are found in your part of the country. For more information, visit www.arc-trust.org.

- Take part in an organised walk to see and hear Natterjack Toads; take part in a habitat conservation work at a Natterjack Toad site; offer to help monitor a site near you; help fund the creation of a Natterjack Toad pond.

NORTH ATLANTIC RIGHT WHALE

'SADLY, IT WAS BEING THE "RIGHT" WHALE TO HUNT THAT HAS DRIVEN THESE ANIMALS TO NEAR EXTINCTION'
WHALE AND DOLPHIN CONSERVATION (WDC)

The North Atlantic Right Whale is one of the most endangered of the great whales, with their worldwide population estimated at fewer than 400 individuals. Right Whales got their name because whalers considered them to be the 'right' whale to hunt as they are easy to approach and catch, float when dead and have a lot of oil in their blubber, which was sold for many things, including making soap and paint. Sadly, it was being the 'right' whale to hunt that has driven these animals to near extinction.

North Atlantic Right Whales live only along the east coast of North America and Canada. Today, they are threatened by human disturbance, habitat loss, entanglement in fishing gear and collisions with vessels.

The future of this species is under such threat that the loss of a single Right Whale each year may lead to its extinction. Whale and Dolphin Conservation (WDC) is helping to save the North Atlantic Right Whale by working to reduce deaths in fishing gear, and campaigning for regulations to reduce vessel strikes. Although it is no longer a target for hunters, other species are. WDC also campaigns to end the needless and inhumane killing of all whales in commercial hunts.

COMMON NAME: North Atlantic Right Whale

SCIENTIFIC NAME: *Eubalaena glacialis*

STATUS: Endangered.

SIZE: These animals weigh around one tonne at birth, and grow to 30-80 tonnes. An adult whale is usually 14-17m long.

POPULATION: It is estimated that there are fewer than 400 individual North Atlantic Right Whales in existence.

RANGE: North Atlantic Right Whales live only in the North Atlantic, and the vast majority of them are found in the western North Atlantic, off the coasts of North America and Canada. Only a few individuals are thought to remain in the eastern North Atlantic or may be animals that wander from the western Atlantic.

THREATS: Entanglement in fishing gear, collision with ships, habitat loss, human disturbance and pollution.

 **WDC** WHALE AND DOLPHIN CONSERVATION WHAT YOU CAN DO...

- Become a supporter of WDC and help species such as the North Atlantic Right Whale. Visit www.whales.org.uk for further information.

- You can support WDC by adopting a whale or dolphin, by becoming a member or by signing up to a campaign. For more details on the work of WDC and how you can help, log on to www.whales.org.uk or email info@whales.org.uk.

NUMBAT

'TO SAVE THE NUMBAT FROM EXTINCTION WE NEED TO ESTABLISH REINTRODUCED POPULATIONS IN AREAS SECURE FROM PREDATION BY INTRODUCED FOXES AND CATS'
AUSTRALIAN WILDLIFE TRUST

Bold alternating stripes across the Numbat's back makes it one of Australia's most striking marsupials. It's also one of the few smaller marsupials to be active only during the day, instead of at night. The Numbat feeds on termites exclusively, using its sharp claws to scratch through earth and wood to reach its prey, which it then catches using its long, sticky tongue. At night, it shelters in tree hollows, fallen timber or burrows.

The Numbat once ranged across much of southern Australia. But by the 1980s, it had disappeared from almost its entire range, surviving only in small fragmented populations in south-western Australia. Today, there are only an estimated 750 Numbats left.

The primary driver of its disappearance has been predation by foxes and cats. Their impact in Australia has been catastrophic – they have been the main contributor to the extinction of 22 species of native mammals. To curb this tide of extinctions, Australian Wildlife Trust (AWT) has supported two projects implemented by the non-profit Australian Wildlife Conservancy (AWC), including the construction of the largest fox- and cat-free area on mainland Australia at Scotia Sanctuary in New South Wales. There, and at Yookamurra Sanctuary in South Australia, the Numbat has been reintroduced with great success. These two AWC properties now protect around 33% of the world population of Numbats.

COMMON NAME: Numbat

SCIENTIFIC NAME: *Myrmecobius fasciatus*

SIZE: Up to 45cm in length including tail.

STATUS: Endangered.

POPULATION: About 750 adults.

LIFESPAN: Five to six years in captivity, shorter in the wild.

RANGE: Once across much of southern Australia from western New South Wales and Victoria to Western Australia, as far north as the southern portion of the Northern Territory. Following the introduction of foxes and cats, the range contracted to two small isolated populations in south-western Australia. It has since been reintroduced by AWC to Scotia and Yookamurra Sanctuaries in NSW and SA respectively.

THREATS: Feral cats and foxes.

AUSTRALIAN WILDLIFE TRUST

WHAT YOU CAN DO...

- Support AWT (www.auswildlifetrust.org), a non-profit private organisation, in its mission to assist in the acquisition of land for the conservation of threatened species and ecosystems in Australia.

- Donate to the Mt Gibson Endangered Wildlife Restoration Project (www.australianwildlife.org/AWC-Sanctuaries/Mt-Gibson-Sanctuary.aspx), an initiative by AWT's partner organisation, AWC. This will provide a secure future for more than 10% of Australia's threatened mammal species, including the Numbat. Or visit Mt Gibson when the project opens to the public.

OCEANIC WHITETIP SHARK

'OCEANIC WHITETIPS ARE SUBJECT TO FISHING PRESSURE THROUGHOUT THEIR ENTIRE RANGE AND ARE CAUGHT IN LARGE NUMBERS AS BYCATCH IN PELAGIC LONGLINE FISHERIES'

THE SHARK TRUST

The Oceanic Whitetip is one of the most wide-ranging sharks, found in all tropical and subtropical waters, usually far offshore in waters more than 200m deep. Reaching up to 4m in length, the Oceanic Whitetip is a slow-moving albeit active predator in both daytime and at night, feeding primarily on bony fishes and cephalopods – and to a lesser extent, seabirds, marine mammals, stingrays, carrion and even garbage. Like most sharks, the Oceanic Whitetip is slow-growing and exhibits late maturity (up to seven years for females), a long gestation period (10-12 months) and produces few young (on average five to six pups every two years) – characteristics which make the species highly vulnerable to overfishing.

Oceanic Whitetips are subject to fishing pressure throughout their entire range and are caught in large numbers as bycatch in pelagic longline fisheries. Surveys in the Gulf of Mexico estimate a decline of 99%, while declines of up to 70% and 93% have been reported in the North-west Atlantic and Central Pacific respectively. The central driver behind Oceanic Whitetip mortality is the international demand for shark fins, with the species being one of six sharks most frequently found in the global fin trade. Working at UK and EU levels, and through international conventions and Regional Fisheries Management Organisations, the Shark Trust continues to advocate for effective management and protection of Oceanic Whitetip Shark populations.

COMMON NAME: Oceanic Whitetip Shark

SCIENTIFIC NAME: *Carcharhinus longimanus*

SIZE: Average 2m length, but can be up to 4m.

STATUS: Vulnerable globally, with North-west and Western Central Atlantic populations considered critically endangered. Listed in CITES Appendix II.

POPULATION: Population estimates are difficult to establish for highly migratory, oceanic sharks. Surveys in the Central Pacific, North-west Atlantic and Gulf of Mexico indicate the species has suffered significant declines in abundance.

LIFESPAN: Estimated at 11-13 years; possibly up to 17 years.

RANGE: The Oceanic Whitetip Shark is widespread in tropical, subtropical and temperate waters worldwide, to about 30 degrees latitude.

THREATS: Continued fishing pressure – particularly as bycatch in pelagic longline and purse seine fisheries targeting tuna and swordfish. The Oceanic Whitetip's large fins are highly valued in the global shark fin trade.

WHAT YOU CAN DO...

- Learn more about the Oceanic Whitetip Shark and its conservation status by downloading the Shark Trust factsheet at www.sharktrust.org/factsheets. Record Oceanic Whitetip sightings at www.sharktrust.org/sightings.

- Find out more about the only UK charity dedicated to the conservation of sharks, skates and rays – visit the Shark Trust at www.sharktrust.org.

ORANGUTAN

'AS THE TROPICAL FORESTS OF BORNEO AND SUMATRA CONTINUE
TO BE DESTROYED, THESE SPECIES AND COUNTLESS OTHERS ARE
BEING PUSHED EVER CLOSER AND CLOSER TO EXTINCTION'
ORANGUTAN FOUNDATION

About a million years ago, Orangutans lived throughout much of Asia. Today, their range is much reduced and they are only found in the rapidly disappearing rainforests of Borneo and Sumatra.

The decline of both species is directly related to habitat loss and the primary driver of this is rainforest clearance for oil palm plantations. Logging, mining and forest fires also pose significant threats to the survival of the species. Many experts believe that of all the great apes, the Sumatran Orangutan risks being the first to become extinct in the wild unless immediate action is taken to halt the loss of their precious habitat.

The close relationship between the Orangutan and its rainforest home is a highly complex and interdependent one. Much is still to be learnt about this gentle ape, but we do know that the more we lose of the rainforest, the greater the risk that the Orangutan, one of our closest living relatives, will disappear as well.

COMMON NAME: Bornean Orangutan and Sumatran Orangutan

SCIENTIFIC NAME: *Pongo pygmaeus* and *Pongo abelii*

SIZE: Males average 97cm in height, females 78cm.

STATUS: Endangered (Bornean Orangutan); Critically Endangered (Sumatran Orangutan).

POPULATION: Bornean orangutan has less than 54,000 individuals and the Sumatran species has 6,600 individuals.

LIFESPAN: Up to 45 years in the wild.

RANGE: Borneo and northern Sumatra.

THREATS: The rapid spread of palm oil plantations encroaching upon tropical rainforests. Illegal and poorly managed logging within the same forests.

ORANGUTAN FOUNDATION
A FUTURE FOR ORANGUTANS, FORESTS & PEOPLE

WHAT YOU CAN DO...

- Become a member of, or make a donation to support, the Orangutan Foundation.
- See Orangutans in the wild on a tour in support of the Orangutan Foundation.
- Visit www.orangutan.org.uk or call 020 7724 2912.
- Avoid products that use palm oil. From 2015, in the EU, food products that contain palm oil will be so labelled.

PAINTED DOG

'PAINTED DOGS ARE A FLAGSHIP SPECIES THAT NEED HABITAT AND OUR SUPPORT TO SURVIVE'
PAINTED DOG CONSERVATION

Painted Dogs are the sole representatives of a unique evolutionary line and therefore rank high for conservation. At the turn of the 20th century the population was estimated to be 500,000. Because of prejudice against predators and misunderstanding of their important role in ecosystems, they were incorrectly labelled as putative stock killers and slaughtered in their thousands. Today their greatest threats are loss of quality prey-rich habitat and poachers' snares, with many also getting run over by speeding vehicles.

Every Painted Dog has a coat pattern comprising of gold, white and black that is as unique as a fingerprint. They are highly social and rarely show any aggression to other pack members. They are also nature's most caring carnivore, caring for old, sick and injured pack members, by feeding them and licking wounds to help them heal. They also allow their pups to feed first and will bring food back to any pack member that is too old to hunt or is undertaking baby-sitting duties.

Because of their incredible teamwork where every dog has a job during the hunt or protecting the pups, the loss of just one adult pack member can spell doom for the entire pack.

Their territories average 750km², thus they need vast protected areas, as well as human tolerance and understanding if they are to survive and flourish.

COMMON NAME: Painted Dog, African Wild Dog, Hunting Dog

SCIENTIFIC NAME: *Lycaon pictus*. Translates as 'painted wolf-like animal'.

SIZE: Up to 1.4m in length, with a tail of up to 45cm. Height at shoulder 75cm.

STATUS: Endangered

POPULATION: 4,000 to 7,000 left in the wild.

LIFESPAN: 7 to 12 years in the wild.

RANGE: Sub-Saharan Africa – only seven of the original 39 range countries in Africa now hold potentially viable populations.

THREATS: Loss of habitat, speeding cars, illegal snares set by poachers for bushmeat. Also in some livestock areas, the dogs are often wrongly blamed for livestock loss and deliberately poisoned or shot.

WHAT YOU CAN DO...

- Raise awareness of the plight of the Painted Dogs and find more information about the species and required conservation work by visiting Painted Dog Conservation at www.painteddog.org.

- Become a friend of painted dogs, support through fundraising events or by making a direct donation. Contact info@painteddog.org.

PHILIPPINE EAGLE OWL

'AS BY FAR THE LARGEST OWL IN THE PHILIPPINES, THIS OWL IS AT THE TOP OF THE FOOD PYRAMID, AND AS SUCH IS EXTREMELY VULNERABLE TO THE LOSS OF ITS HABITAT'
WORLD OWL TRUST

The Philippines has more threatened owls than any other country in the world, due to the destruction of virtually all the lowland rainforest, which once covered 75% of the low-lying areas of the country – the home of most Philippine owls and many other species of flora and fauna. This owl is at the top of the food pyramid, and as such is extremely vulnerable to the loss of its habitat – lowland forest near watercourses.

Always uncommon, the Philippine Eagle Owl has been recorded from six islands in the past, but the few recent records have all been made in the Sierra Madre mountains of Luzon and only number three to four individuals at three sites.

The World Owl Trust has entered into a Memorandum of Agreement with the Philippine government to set up and manage the Philippine Owl Conservation Programme – the first international owl conservation programme aimed at saving not only endangered Philippine owls, such as the Philippine Eagle Owl, but also the country's overall biodiversity.

COMMON NAME:
Philippine Eagle Owl
SCIENTIFIC NAME:
Bubo philippensis
SIZE: Up to 50cm long, wingspan about 35cm.
STATUS: Endangered
POPULATION: Unknown, but certainly declining rapidly.
LIFESPAN: Unknown, but probably around 25 years.
RANGE: Formerly recorded from six (possibly seven) Philippine islands, but recent records only from northern Luzon.
THREATS: Severe deforestation of lowland tropical rainforests throughout the Philippines, plus probable persecution.

WHAT YOU CAN DO...

- Join the World Owl Trust online at www.owls.org and click the shop link or telephone 01229 717393.

- Make a donation directly to the trust online at www.owls.org and click the just giving link or by just text giving, text WOTC40 plus your amount to 70070, texts are free. Find us on Facebook.

PINE MARTEN

'PINE MARTENS STILL REMAIN ONE OF THE RAREST NATIVE
MAMMALS IN GREAT BRITAIN, WITH A TOTAL POPULATION
OF AROUND 3,000 TO 4,000'
THE MAMMAL SOCIETY

The Pine Marten, one of Britain's rarest and most elusive native mammals, was widespread throughout much of mainland Britain and some of the Scottish islands as little as 200 years ago.

Habitat fragmentation, persecution by gamekeepers and being killed for their fur drastically reduced this distribution. By 1926, their last remaining stronghold was restricted to a small area of north-west Scotland, with small numbers in north Wales and the Lake District.

They have now increased their range in Scotland and are found to occur in the same parts of England and Wales. Conservationists were ecstatic at the news of a male recently found in 2012 as roadkill near Newtown, Powys, which was the first confirmed sighting of the species in Wales since 1971.

Despite this good news, Pine Martens still remain one of the rarest native mammals in the UK, with a total population of around 3,000 to 4,000. They face continued threats of urbanisation, habitat fragmentation in the lowlands and increased density of roads. Conservation strategies, such as planting corridors of trees between patches of suitable habitat and reintroductions to England, have been proposed, but feasibility studies, funding and more precise details of the requirements of this species are required before any reintroductions occur.

COMMON NAME: Pine Marten

SCIENTIFIC NAME: *Martes martes*

SIZE: Up to 53cm in length, with tail up to 25cm.

STATUS: Threatened. The Pine Marten is classified as Least Concern on the IUCN Red List, and is listed on Schedule 5 of the Wildlife and Countryside Act 1981, and Schedule 3 of The Conservation Regulations 1994.

POPULATION: In the UK, the Pine Marten is restricted to the Scottish Highlands and Grampian, and a few populations occur in southern Scotland.

LIFESPAN: Eighteen years in captivity, but in the wild a lifespan of eight to 10 years is more typical.

RANGE: Although Pine Martens are distributed throughout much of Europe, in the UK they are now rare. Pine Martens are now rare. They were formerly widely distributed in Britain, but are now mostly confined to Galloway and the north-west of Scotland.

THREATS: Persecution (illegal poisoning and shooting) by gamekeepers; hunting for their fine fur; and loss of habitat leading to fragmentation.

THE Mammal SOCIETY

WHAT YOU CAN DO...

- Support charities and organisations working for the conservation of the Pine Marten, such as The Mammal Society (www.mammal.org.uk), MISE Project (www.miseproject.ie) and The Vincent Wildlife Trust (www.vwt.org.uk).

- If you think you have seen a Pine Marten in England or Wales, we would love to hear about it. Please call 023 8023 7874 and submit your records to our National Mammal Atlas Project.

PIPING PLOVER

'THE PERMANENT PROTECTION OF KEY SHORELINE BREEDING
AREAS IS CRITICAL TO THE SURVIVAL OF THE PIPING PLOVER'
NATURE CONSERVANCY CANADA

Soon after birth, downy Piping Plover chicks are able to follow their parents looking for insects and worms in the sand, but their chances of survival are slim. These endangered shorebirds lay their eggs on the ground, often on the same beaches frequented by humans.

The eggs and young are so well camouflaged that they are often not noticed until they have been trampled or crushed by off-road vehicles. The eggs are further threatened by changes in water levels due to building activities, dams and storms. The fledglings, unable to fly for their first 30 days, are appetising to cats and dogs, and other predators such as gulls and raccoons, attracted by picnickers' litter.

With only 6,000 adult Piping Plovers remaining worldwide, the permanent protection of key shoreline breeding areas is now critical to the survival of this tiny bird.

COMMON NAME: Piping Plover

SCIENTIFIC NAME: *Charadrius melodus*

SIZE: Up to 19cm long, wingspan 35-41cm.

STATUS: Endangered in the US and Canada.

POPULATION: The worldwide population is estimated at 6,000 adults. The Canadian Atlantic populations of the melodus subspecies consists of fewer than 500 individuals.

LIFESPAN: Only 13% of females and 28% of males live five years. Maximum age is 11.

RANGE: Piping plovers breed in the Great Plains, on the North American Atlantic coast, in the Great Lakes and in St Pierre et Miquelon. Winters from North Carolina to Florida, in the Gulf States, Mexico and the Caribbean.

THREATS: Destruction and degradation of habitat, human use of beaches, predation, shoreline erosion, nest destruction and changes in water levels.

NATURE CONSERVANCY CANADA

WHAT YOU CAN DO...

- Protect critical remaining Piping Plover habitat on the Great Plains and Atlantic coast by contributing to Nature Conservancy Canada (NCC) at www.natureconservancy.ca. NCC works to protect Piping Plover habitat by acquiring and permanently protecting the beaches they use for breeding.

- Obey signs posted to protect Piping Plovers and do not approach their nests. Be careful to properly dispose of all litter when outdoors. When on beaches used by Piping Plovers, keep your pets on a lead.

POLAR BEAR

'DISAPPEARING ICE FLOES ROB POLAR BEARS OF THEIR HUNTING GROUNDS, LEAVING THEM TOO THINLY SPREAD TO REPRODUCE'
NATURE CANADA

Polar Bears are the world's largest land predators, and the most majestic creatures of the far north. But dramatic changes taking place in the Arctic threaten the survival of this spectacular species.

Global warming is melting the polar ice caps, robbing the bears of the ice floes they need to hunt prey. As the annual sea-ice melts, Polar Bears are forced ashore to spend their summers fasting. If the Arctic ice cap continues to melt sooner and form later, Polar Bears will become too thinly spread to reproduce and they'll be extinct by the end of this century.

Increased human activity in the north brings other threats to the Polar Bear. Because they are at the top of the food chain, Polar Bears are highly exposed to toxic chemicals ingested by the animals they eat.

As shipping traffic increases in the north, spilled oil strips the bear's fur of its insulating properties, and renders the bear's prey inedible.

Thanks in part to campaigning and petitioning by Nature Canada, the polar bear has been listed as a species of special concern. By continuing to raise awareness of the effects of climate change upon the polar bear and its habitat, Nature Canada hopes to be able to play a part in slowing down the rate of global warming, giving the population of this impressive bear a chance to stabilise.

COMMON NAME: Polar Bear

SCIENTIFIC NAME: *Ursus maritimus*

SIZE: 2-3m in length.

STATUS: Vulnerable.

POPULATION:
About 22,000 to 27,000.

LIFESPAN: 20-25 years.

RANGE: Most polar bears live in Canada, but other populations exist in Alaska, Russia, Greenland and Norway (Svalbard).

THREATS: Air pollution, climate change, oil spills and toxic chemicals.

WHAT YOU CAN DO...

- Support Nature Canada's efforts to save the Polar Bear's habitat by making a donation at www.naturecanada.ca. Nature Canada is working to protect Canada's far north from industrialisation and the effects of global warming.

- Climate change affects humans and bears alike. Do your part to slow global warming. Visit www.naturecanada.ca to find out how.

PONDS

'THERE ARE ABOUT 478,000 PONDS LEFT IN GREAT BRITAIN, COMPARED WITH 1.2 MILLION IN 1880'
POND CONSERVATION

Whether in towns and villages or out in the countryside, ponds are exceptionally rich wildlife habitats, and can provide stepping stones for many species that use freshwater habitats to move across the landscape. Typically, ponds support around 70% of the freshwater species found in lowland landscapes, including more of the most endangered species than either rivers, lakes or ditches. And ponds pack all this biodiversity into a tiny space: only 5% of the water area taken up by lakes, rivers, streams and ditches.

During the 20th century large numbers of ponds were destroyed, and over half of the ponds that existed at the beginning of the 20th century are now gone. This is mostly due to drainage or infilling for agricultural purposes, although destruction for urban development has also played a part.

Worse still, there is evidence of a decline in pond quality in the past 10 years, linked to high nutrient levels and the damaging influences of road run-off and polluted inflows. Ponds are particularly vulnerable to pollution because of their small size and the low volume of water available to dilute pollutants.

Pond creation is a simple, cheap and effective way to bring back clean water to the countryside, and help safeguard our endangered freshwater wildlife.

COMMON NAME: Ponds can also be called pools, tarns or lochans.

STATUS: Ponds declined greatly in numbers and quality during the 20th century.

POPULATION: There are about 478,000 ponds left in Great Britain, compared with 1.2 million in 1880. This decline is likely to be typical of most industrialised countries.

LIFESPAN: Most ponds today were probably made in the past 500 years, although some date from the ice age about 10,000 years ago.

RANGE: Pond Conservation defines a pond as a body of water (normally fresh water, but occasionally brackish) that can vary in size between 1m^2 and 2ha (about 2.5 football pitches), and which holds water for four months of the year or more.

THREATS: Habitat destruction through urban development. Pollution from road run-off, acid rain, polluted inflows and intensive farming.

Pond
Conservation
For life in fresh waters

WHAT YOU CAN DO...

- Create a wildlife pond in your garden. For a step-by-step guide, download *Creating Garden Ponds for Wildlife* from Pond Conservation's website at: www.pondconservation.org.uk/advice/makingpondsforwildlife.

- Get involved with Pond Conservation. Visit www.pondconservation.org.uk/supportus/joinus. Become a pond protector and receive monthly e-updates regarding ponds and other freshwater habitats, access to specialised advice and practical opportunities to get involved with their work.

PYGMY HOG

'THE WORLD'S SMALLEST PIG IS NOW FOUND ONLY IN ASSAM, WHERE A POPULATION OF AROUND 500 ANIMALS MAY EXIST'
DURRELL WILDLIFE CONSERVATION TRUST

The Pygmy Hog is the world's smallest pig, with adults reaching a weight of less than 10kg. They once occurred in tall grasslands from Nepal and Bhutan to Assam in north-east India. However, they are now known to be found only in the Manas Tiger Reserve in Assam, where a population of around 500 animals may exist.

Habitat loss through uncontrolled burning of the tall grasslands is thought to have been the cause for the species' disappearance throughout most of its former range. These diminutive pigs rely on the thatch for cover from predators, for food and, uniquely, for the building of their nests for breeding.

Durrell has established a very successful captive breeding programme and plans to release Pygmy Hogs into protected areas in which they once occurred. Animals will be radio-tracked and monitored to learn more about their home ranges and use of habitat. Durrell also works in conjunction with the Assamese and Indian forestry departments in securing the future for this species and other biodiversity of the region.

COMMON NAME: Pygmy Hog
SCIENTIFIC NAME: *Sus salvanius*
SIZE: Male 61-71cm in length. Female 55-62 cm.
STATUS: Critically Endangered.
LIFESPAN: More than 10 years.
POPULATION: Unknown, but presumed to be fewer than 500 animals in the wild.
RANGE: Now known to be found only in the Manas Tiger Reserve in Assam.
THREATS: Habitat destruction through uncontrolled burning of the tall grasslands which they rely on for cover from predators, for food and for building their nests.

durrell WHAT YOU CAN DO...

- Help fund the conservation of the Pygmy Hog by becoming a member of Durrell Wildlife Conservation Trust. Join online at www.durrellwildlife.org or write for a membership application form to: Durrell Wildlife Conservation Trust, Les Augrès Manor, La Profonde Rue, Trinity, Jersey JE3 5BP.

- Durrell Wildlife Conservation Trust is the only UK charity working to save the Pygmy Hog. You can help by making a donation to this project, or you can leave a legacy to the trust to help with this and the trust's other projects to save endangered species from extinction.

PYGMY RWANDAN WATER LILY

'CARLOS MAGDALENA, A HORTICULTURIST AT KEW, DISCOVERED THE SECRET OF GROWING THIS UNIQUE AFRICAN WATER LILY, THE SMALLEST SPECIES IN THE WORLD – BRINGING IT BACK FROM THE BRINK OF EXTINCTION'

ROYAL BOTANIC GARDENS, KEW

Nymphaea thermarum is the smallest water lily in the world, now extinct in the wild, and the only one of its kind to grow in mud rather than water. It was discovered in 1987 in south-west Rwanda by German botanist Professor Eberhard Fischer.

Fischer realised that the species was in jeopardy and he transported a few plants to Bonn Botanic Gardens. There, valuable specimens lasted for more than a decade, but their propagation was unsuccessful. In 2009 a handful of seeds and seedlings were sent from Bonn to Kew.

Carlos Magdalena who has a track record of bringing the rarest plants back from the brink, took on the challenge of trying to propagate the water lily. He ran a series of unsuccessful trials, but then returned to the first description of the species that supplied a vital clue: 'it grows in damp mud caused by the overflow of a hot spring...' Carlos placed seeds and seedlings in loam pots in small containers filled with water, keeping the water at the same level as the surface of the compost, at a temperature of 25°C, exposing the seedlings to higher concentrations of carbon dioxide and oxygen in the air. Eight plants began to flourish, growing to maturity and flowering for the first time.

Now that it is easily cultivated at Kew, there is the opportunity to reintroduce *Nymphaea thermarum* to Rwanda.

COMMON NAME: None; at Kew we call it the Pygmy Rwandan Water Lily

SCIENTIFIC NAME: *Nymphaea thermarum*

SIZE: The pads of *N. thermarum* measure only 1cm across.

STATUS: Extinct in the wild.

POPULATION: At present all the extant plants are in cultivation at Kew and in Germany.

LIFESPAN: More than 10 years.

RANGE: Before becoming extinct in the wild, it was found at a single site in Mashyuza, south-west Rwanda (Africa). A tiny water lily, its rosettes are 10-20cm wide, comprising bright green lily pads that can be as little as 1cm in diameter. Its habitat is mud created by the overflow of a freshwater hot spring, where the water has cooled to 25°C.

THREATS: The only population of this species died out as a consequence of over-exploitation of the aquifer that fed the hot spring that kept the plants moist and at a constant temperature.

WHAT YOU CAN DO...

- Support Kew's Millennium Seed Bank Partnership, which has successfully banked seeds from 10% of the world's wild plant species and is aiming on saving 25% by 2020.

- Become involved by adopting a seed, or get together with friends to save a plant species and know that you have played a vital part in protecting our environment.

- Find out more about this work and our Breathing Planet Campaign at www.kew.org/support-kew.

RAINFOREST

'THE EARTH'S SINGLE GREATEST BIOLOGICAL TREASURE BANK: START SAVING NOW'
WORLD LAND TRUST

Tropical forests have evolved over millions of years to become the store of living and breathing renewable natural resources that they are today. Scientists estimate that more than half of all the world's plant and animal species live in tropical forests.

Not only are they important hotspots for biodiversity, they perform a variety of different ecological services essential for the human population. Rainforests are important for the purification of water supplies in many areas, absorb air pollution and also produce roughly 40% of the Earth's oxygen. Climate change is perhaps the biggest environmental threat facing the planet and saving tropical forests will lock up carbon, helping to offset the damage caused by modern-day living.

The World Land Trust (WLT) works with in-country partner NGOs to save tropical forests and other threatened habitats through the creation of protected reserves and restoration of degraded habitats, and supports the ongoing protection of reserves through funding local rangers. Since 1989, WLT and its local partners have purchased and restored more than 16,000ha of threatened habitats, which would otherwise have been lost for ever. WLT has also been instrumental in planting more than a million trees to date, and now also funds 20 rangers worldwide to ensure the ongoing protection of tropical forests and other threatened habitats.

RANGE: Central and South America, West and Central Africa, eastern Madagascar, Assam, India, South-east Asia, New Guinea and Queensland, Australia.

SIZE: Rainforests once covered 14% of the Earth's land surface, now they are reduced to less than 6%.

TROPICAL FOREST SPECIES: The most diverse ecosystems, it is estimated that a 10km² area of rainforest could contain as many as 1,500 species of flowering plants, 750 species of trees, 125 species of mammals, 400 species of birds, 100 species of reptiles, 60 species of amphibian and 150 species of butterflies.

THREATS: The main threats to tropical forests come from commercial logging and mining activities, migrant cultivation (slash and burn), conversion to agricultural land, mono-culture plantations (for example, oil palm and soya), cattle pasture and demand for fuel wood.

 WORLD LAND TRUST™ WHAT YOU CAN DO...

- Visit www.worldlandtrust.org to buy an acre of rainforest and help local organisations to create reserves to ensure the protection of threatened habitats in perpetuity.

- Support the ongoing protection of tropical forests by donating to the Keepers of the Wild programme, funding salaries and equipment of rangers in the field, to prevent illegal logging and poaching.

- Become a Friend of World Land Trust at www.worldlandtrust.org and your monthly donations will help WLT respond quickly

RED RUFFED LEMUR

'UNLESS THE ISLAND IS STABILISED QUICKLY, EXTINCTION OF LEMURS IN THE WILD ON MADAGASCAR IS A REAL POSSIBILITY IN THE NEXT 50-60 YEARS'
LEMUR CONSERVATION FOUNDATION

Red Ruffed Lemurs are among the most exquisite and charismatic of the endangered lemurs. Madagascar, home to all lemurs, is considered one of the most ecologically diverse and important regions on the planet. However, the island has lost about 90% of its forest since the arrival of humans more than 2,000 years ago. In north-eastern Madagascar, illegal logging of precious hardwoods, such as rosewood and ebony, in the Masoala National Park has dramatically increased in the aftermath of the 2009 government coup, causing an increase in the threats faced by the Red Ruffed Lemurs' natural habitat.

This severe loss of habitat, the hunting of lemurs for food, and some lemurs categorised as crop pests has made lemurs the most threatened mammal in the world in 2012. The Red Ruffed Lemurs, one of the top 25 most endangered primates, are restricted to only one small region of Madagascar and suffer the same threats as other lemurs.

Current changes under way to stem this loss give some reason for hope, but unless the island is stabilised quickly, extinction of lemurs in the wild on Madagascar is a real possibility in the next 50-60 years.

COMMON NAME: Red Ruffed Lemur

SCIENTIFIC NAME: *Varecia rubra*

SIZE: Body up to 53cm in length. Tail up to 60cm.

STATUS: Critically Endangered.

POPULATION: According to a 1997 survey, there were about 15,000 Red Ruffed Lemurs of breeding age in the wild.

LIFESPAN: 15-20 years in the wild.

RANGE: Red Ruffed Lemurs live in a very restricted area, mostly in the Masoala National Park (235,580ha) on the Masoala Peninsula in north-eastern Madagascar. Within that region, Red Ruffed Lemurs have home ranges of about 58ha.

THREATS: Red Ruffed Lemurs are losing their habitat, they are hunted for food and are subject to severe environmental distress, such as cyclones, which often hit this area of Madagascar.

LEMUR CONSERVATION FOUNDATION

WHAT YOU CAN DO...

- Sign up for their conservation newsletter and discover what the Lemur Conservation Foundation is doing to help conserve red ruffed and other lemurs, by visiting www.lemurreserve.org.

- Be aware of the source of any tropical hardwoods you buy; make sure your purchase does not contribute to the illegal trade from deforestation of Madagascar habitats.

RED SQUIRREL

'SINCE 1952, A STAGGERING 95% OF RED SQUIRRELS HAVE BEEN WIPED OUT IN ENGLAND AND WALES. UNLESS URGENT ACTION IS TAKEN, THE SAME FATE COULD BEFALL SCOTLAND'S RED SQUIRREL POPULATION'
SCOTTISH WILDLIFE TRUST

Fifty years ago, the Red Squirrel was a common sight in Scotland. But today, the Red Squirrel is facing an uncertain future. The vast woodlands it once called home are diminished and fragmented. The Grey Squirrel – introduced from North America in the 1870s as a Victorian curiosity – threatens the supply of food.

Worse still, squirrel pox, a deadly virus carried by Greys, is spreading. The disease kills almost 100% of the Red Squirrels it comes into contact with and there is no cure. In 2007, it reached Scotland. If squirrel pox spreads at the same rate as it has in parts of England (where an alarming 95% of Reds have been wiped out since 1952), the virus could reach the Highlands in as little as 10 years.

With three-quarters of the UK's remaining Red Squirrel population found in Scotland, the Scottish Wildlife Trust is taking action to address the decline of this Scottish icon.

In the south, we are engaged in efforts to halt the spread of squirrel pox. Further north, we are stopping the Reds' decline by reducing Grey Squirrel numbers in key areas, such as Loch Lomond, Perthshire, Angus and Aberdeen. Our efforts have seen Red Squirrels return to parts of the Borders, Tayside and Aberdeenshire where they have not been seen for years.

There is still much to do, but with your help the Red Squirrel has the chance to become a true conservation success story.

COMMON NAME: Eurasian Red Squirrel

SCIENTIFIC NAME: *Sciurus vulgaris*

SIZE: Up to 23cm in length, with a tail length of 15-20cm.

STATUS: Vulnerable and Conservation Dependent in Scotland

POPULATION: According to a 1995 estimate, there were about 121,000 Red Squirrels in Scotland.

LIFESPAN: Five to seven years in the wild.

RANGE: Widely spread in Scotland, but now largely absent from the Central Lowlands, Ayrshire and much of the Borders, and declining in Dumfries and Galloway. Very localised in small pockets in the rest of the UK.

THREATS: Replacement by the invasive non-native Grey Squirrel, which competes more successfully for the same food and living space, and is a reservoir of the squirrel pox virus, which transmits readily (and fatally) to Red Squirrels.

Scottish Wildlife Trust

WHAT YOU CAN DO...

- By joining the Scottish Wildlife Trust, you can save an entire species from extinction in Scotland, and help us protect the Red Squirrel against the many threats it faces. Visit www.scottishwildlifetrust.org.uk/join for details.

- Report your squirrel sightings (both Red and Grey) in Scotland via our website: www.scottishwildlifetrust.org.uk/reportsquirrel

RED-BREASTED GOOSE

'THE RED-BREASTED GOOSE IS CURRENTLY LISTED AS THE MOST
THREATENED GOOSE SPECIES ON THE IUCN LIST DUE TO ITS
POPULATION CRASH IN THE EARLY 2000s'
BULGARIAN SOCIETY FOR THE PROTECTION OF BIRDS

The Red-breasted Goose is one of the most enigmatic waterbirds in Eurasia.
Until the 1950s, this Arctic breeder used to winter along the Caspian coast
in Azerbaijan, but land use changes led to a crash in population and shifted
the wintering grounds to the north-western Black Sea coast in Ukraine,
Romania and Bulgaria. The population slowly recovered, building up
to 88,000 birds in the late 1990s, concentrated in winter in a relatively
small area in Romania and Bulgaria. However, the population declined
dramatically in the early 2000s, reducing to fewer than 40,000 birds.

The species faces serious threats along its almost 6,000km long journey
to its wintering habitats: though legally protected in all countries, the Red-
breasts are shot at along the migration route by poachers; changes in land
use practices have reduced food availability; disturbance of feeding birds
by hunters in vehicles has affected foraging and prenuptial accumulation of
fat reserves, affecting survival during spring migration and breeding; there
are indications that wind farm developments in Romania and Bulgaria have
displaced foraging flocks; and climate change and associated habitat shifts
are also expected to have a negative impact. Modelling indicates that 67%
of the habitat for this species could be lost by 2070.

The BSPB is now leading a big EU LIFE+ Project in partnership with
WWT and RSPB, and local farmers and hunters to improve understanding
of species ecology and promoting appropriate farming practices, managed
hunting and spatial planning in coastal Dobrudzha in Bulgaria.

COMMON NAME:
Red-breasted Goose

SCIENTIFIC NAME: *Branta ruficollis*

SIZE: 53-56 cm in length.

STATUS: Endangered Globally (IUCN).

POPULATION: The largest winter
count in recent years was 55,000
birds in January 2013, which is
estimated to be the approximate
current global population.

LIFESPAN: Fifteen years in the wild;
25 in captivity.

RANGE: Breeds in Taimyr, Yamal
and Guidan in Arctic Russia and
migrates along the Ob River through
staging areas in north and north-east
Kazakhstan, Kalmykia and winters in
Ukraine, Romania and Bulgaria where
it concentrates in five to 10 sites.
Vagrant individuals or small flock are
found in other countries in Europe.

THREATS: Relatively small changes
in mortality affect population
levels. Changes in agriculture and
abandonment of grazing is reducing
food availability at staging and
wintering grounds. Wind farms and
other developments are reducing
feeding areas.

WHAT YOU CAN DO...

- You can join our efforts by becoming a member of BSPB. Learn more at www.bspb.org.

- You can support our conservation activities for the Red-breasted Goose with a donation;
  find out more or contact us via www.bspb-redbreasts.org.

ROSEATE TERN

'ONE OF EUROPE'S MOST BEAUTIFUL BREEDING SEABIRDS, THE ROSEATE TERN
IS UNFORTUNATELY ALSO ONE OF ITS RAREST AND MOST THREATENED'
BIRDWATCH IRELAND

In summer, Ireland holds approximately 85% of the north-west European breeding population of 1,450 pairs of Roseate Tern, with more than 1,200 pairs alone on Rockabill Island off the coast of Dublin. The remainder nest in Britain and north-west France, the only other European colonies being in the Azores. It has longer tail-streamers than many other terns, and in the summer adults have a pink blush on their underparts which gives the bird its name.

The main threats facing the Irish population are the exploitation of marine resources and the concentration of the majority of the breeding population, making it vulnerable to single high-impact events, such as an oil spill. The trapping of young birds at their wintering grounds along the coast of west Africa remains of ongoing concern for the survival of the species.

To ensure their future, new colonies must be established outside current breeding strongholds, and feeding grounds near them adequately protected.

COMMON NAME: Roseate Tern

SCIENTIFIC NAME: *Sterna dougallii*

SIZE: Approx 36cm in length with a 76cm wingspan.

STATUS: Red-listed in Ireland, EU Annex 1.

POPULATION: Around 120,000 to 130,000 pairs worldwide; Europe holds 2,000 pairs, confined to Ireland, Britain, France and the Azores.

LIFESPAN: The oldest recorded individual was 25 years old.

RANGE: The threatened *dougallii* subspecies breeds only in the Atlantic, at colonies in Europe, North America, the Caribbean and South Africa. Other races breed in Australia, Japan and at various sites in the Indo-Pacific region.

THREATS: Trapping on wintering grounds, lack of suitable nesting sites, reduction in fish stocks, human disturbance and marine pollution.

BirdWatchIreland
protecting birds and biodiversity

WHAT YOU CAN DO...

- Dublin Bay, on the east coast of Ireland, is one of the best places to see Roseate Terns. If you find a ringed Roseate Tern or ring-read it using a telescope, please report the details of the ring to BirdWatch Ireland to help in the study of the survival rates of the species.

- To find out more about Roseate Terns or to join BirdWatch Ireland and support its conservation work, visit www.birdwatchireland.ie or write to BirdWatch Ireland, Unit 20, Block D, Bullford Business Campus, Kilcoole, Co Wicklow, Ireland.

ROSEWOODS OF MADAGASCAR

'THE UNIQUE ROSEWOOD TREES OF MADAGASCAR ARE BEING LOST
AT AN UNPRECEDENTED RATE TO SATISFY DEMAND FOR THEIR
PRECIOUS TIMBER, WHICH CONTINUES TO DRIVE ILLEGAL LOGGING'
BOTANIC GARDENS CONSERVATION INTERNATIONAL

In 2010, UNESCO added Madagascar's rainforests to its list of 36 sites categorised as World Heritage in Danger. These relict forests are vital for the survival of Madagascar's unique biodiversity. Deforestation has devastated the landscape of Madagascar with only 8.5% of its original forests remaining. There are 48 species of rosewood endemic to Madagascar of which 15 yield superior quality rosewood.

Intensive uncontrolled illegal logging for international trade is being driven by demand for high-quality furniture, guitars and other finished products. A small portion is traded by locals but 95% is illegally exported to China and 5% to USA and European markets. The estimated market value of known exports is in excess of US$227.4 million, with each log worth up to US$1,300.

Removal of trees causes serious degradation of the ecosystem and allows other plant species to invade and colonise, preventing any hope of the rosewoods regrowing. Other endemic island species, particularly primates, are also threatened with extinction as they depend on rosewood trees for shelter and food. Thousands of other trees are destroyed to access the rosewoods and it takes up to eight other tree logs to transport rosewood by river. Areas of forest are cleared to establish camps for loggers.

COMMON NAME: Malagasy Rosewood, Pallisandre

SCIENTIFIC NAME: *Dalbergia spp*

SIZE: 15-23m in height.

STATUS: The 15 most valuable and overexploited species are highly threatened with extinction. CITES Appendix II (2013).

POPULATION: Unknown but declining rapidly as mature and young trees are logged. It has recently been estimated that as many as half a million Rosewood logs are stockpiled in Madagascar awaiting export.

LIFESPAN: Hundreds of years, very slow growth rate of 3mm per year.

RANGE: Many species have undergone range declines by 54-98% and only remain in protected areas in north-west Madagascar.

THREATS: High demand and high prices are driving intensive uncontrolled illegal logging. Poor governance and political upheaval in Madagascar provide no protection even within national parks. There is no seed bank at present, so once this species is gone they are lost for ever.

BGCI
Plants for the Planet

WHAT YOU CAN DO...

- Do not buy any products made from Rosewood unless you are assured that the wood is legally sourced. Check the provisions of CITES.

- If you care about conservation of primates and birds of Madagascar we need to save the forests! Support the conservation activities of your local botanic garden. Visit www.bgci.org/worldwide/get_involved. Find out more about the work of Botanic Gardens Conservation International and the Global Trees Campaign – the world's largest network for plant conservation. Visit www.bgci.org or call +44 (0) 20 8332 5953.

SCALLOPED HAMMERHEAD

'CONTINUED PRESSURE FROM UNREGULATED FISHING HAS SEEN DRAMATIC DECLINES, WITH SCALLOPED HAMMERHEADS BEING SPECIFICALLY TARGETED DUE TO THE VALUE OF FINS'
GALAPAGOS CONSERVATION TRUST

With their distinctive appearance and unusual schooling behaviour, these sharks have intrigued humans for years. The Galapagos Marine Reserve (GMR) remains one of the few places in the world where these animals can still be seen in large aggregations. Divers travel from all over the world for a chance to see this amazing natural spectacle, creating an important alternative income for the local community that does not rely on extraction.

Although sharks are protected within the GMR, the high demand and economic value for shark fins has led to substantial illegal catches. Scalloped Hammerheads are specifically targeted due to their high fin ray count, which increases the value of fins. This species is particularly vulnerable to exploitation due to certain life history characteristics, such as a long gestation period and their aggregating behaviour, and are now considered to be Globally Endangered.

Understanding of the distribution, abundance and behaviour of Scalloped Hammerheads is currently poor, but is critical for their protection. Further research is essential in order to create a baseline for future monitoring.

COMMON NAME: Scalloped Hammerhead

SCIENTIFIC NAME: *Sphyrna lewini*

SIZE: Up to 2.5m in length.

STATUS: Endangered.

POPULATION: Accurate catch data does not exist, but a 50-90% decline has been recorded around the world.

LIFESPAN: Thought to be around 30 years.

RANGE: Circumglobal in warm temperate and tropical seas, although there is genetic evidence for geographic subpopulations.

THREATS: Hammerhead Sharks are specifically targeted in some areas due to their fins being more highly valued than those of other species. In addition to targeted fishing, Hammerhead Sharks are also very vulnerable to bycatch.

Galapagos Conservation Trust

WHAT YOU CAN DO...

- Join the Galapagos Conservation Trust and help to ensure a sustainable future for the Galapagos Islands and the GMR – a conservation model for the world. Visit www.savegalapagos.org for more information.

- Keep the conservation conversation going by learning more about the issues in Galapagos and their global significance – visit our blog galapagosblog.org, join us on Facebook or Twitter (@galapagossip).

SCALY-SIDED MERGANSER

'THIS BEAUTIFUL DUCK REQUIRES CLEAN FAST-FLOWING RIVERS WITH ABUNDANT FISH AND BROAD-LEAF RIVERINE FOREST FOR NESTING IN CAVITIES – HABITATS WHICH ARE BECOMING SCARCE IN DEVELOPING CHINA'
EAST ASIAN-AUSTRALASIAN FLYWAY PARTNERSHIP SCALY-SIDED MERGANSER TASK FORCE

Far eastern Russia, and the Primorye region in particular, have become the last refuge for several endangered species originating from China. Together with the Amur Tiger, the Scaly-sided Merganser is a species that is particularly badly affected by rapid development in China and becoming increasingly dependent on less populated habitats in Russia for survival.

The species' home range is now restricted to just three mountain countries, and any habitat loss via deforestation, river pollution or overfishing has a critical impact on its small global population. A Scaly-sided Merganser Task Force study found that the life expectancy of breeding females is now very short – probably as a result of hunting and of bycatch in fishing nets. Genetic diversity of the species is among the lowest of all world bird species.

However, information and education programmes with local people within the breeding range promise to help decrease direct bird mortality; and artificial nest programmes can be effective in compensating for breeding habitat loss due to the logging of riverine forests. As annual productivity is a key factor for the species' survival, the EAAFP Scaly-sided Merganser Task Force is researching construction techniques for artificial nests, which will render them both attractive to ducks and predator safe. Unfortunately, winter habitat degradation, due both to dam building and river pollution from industrial development in China, is difficult to mitigate.

COMMON NAME:
Scaly-sided Merganser
SCIENTIFIC NAME:
Mergus squamatus
SIZE: Approx 58cm in length.
STATUS: Endangered.
POPULATION: 4,600 individuals.
LIFESPAN: No females studied lived longer than eight years – unusually short for a sea duck species.
RANGE: Breeds entirely in far eastern Russia and north-east China within two mountain ranges: Sikhote-Alin in Russia and Changbai in China and DPR Korea, providing home for 98% of the world population. Winters mainly on the tributaries of the Yangtze river in China; in fewer numbers in South Korea, and a very few in Japan, Vietnam and Taiwan.
THREATS: Breeding and wintering habitat degradation in China; illegal shooting during duck spring season; and mortality in illegal fish nets in the rivers of Russia.

EAAFP

WHAT YOU CAN DO...

- Discover what the Scaly-sided Merganser Projects (both in Russia and China) are doing to help conserve the Scaly-sided Merganser by visiting www.eaaflyway.net/scaly-sided-merganser.php.

- Be aware of the source of any boreal hardwoods you buy. Make sure your purchase does not contribute to the illegal trade from deforestation of far eastern Russia's broad-leaved forests.

- Support the work of the Scaly-sided Merganser Projects via WWT by becoming a WWT member at www.wwt.org.uk.

SCIMITAR-HORNED ORYX

'THESE IMPRESSIVE ANTELOPE ARE PERFECTLY ADAPTED TO THEIR ARID HABITAT, BUT HAVE BEEN DRIVEN TO EXTINCTION BY OVER-HUNTING AND COMPETITION WITH DOMESTIC LIVESTOCK'

MARWELL WILDLIFE

Scimitar-horned Oryx were one of the last species of large mammal to become extinct in the wild in the late-20th century. These impressive antelopes are perfectly adapted to the semi-arid grasslands that surround the great Sahara Desert, and tens of thousands used to join together in large annual migrations after the rains in search of fresh pasture. Excessive hunting, competition with domestic livestock and prolonged droughts caused their decline, and then extinction in the wild, across their historic range.

Luckily, by the time the last remaining wild population disappeared, conservation initiatives were under way, with large numbers maintained in captivity. In 1985, a project began to reintroduce the Oryx to Bou-Hedma National Park in Tunisia, and today Oryx have been released to fenced protected areas in three other parks in Tunisia, and to three parks and reserves in Morocco and Senegal. Plans are currently being developed to carry out a large-scale release of Oryx to Chad. If this project goes ahead, then we may once again see free-ranging Scimitar-horned Oryx in their natural habitat, migrating across the vast Sahel grasslands in search of fresh pasture.

COMMON NAME: Scimitar-horned Oryx

SCIENTIFIC NAME: *Oryx dammah*

SIZE: Males can weigh up to 165kg and females up to 150kg. Males can reach up to 126cm at the shoulder, females up to 120cm.

STATUS: Extinct in the wild.

POPULATION: Reintroductions to fenced protected areas have resulted in approximately 450 individuals in national parks in northern Africa. There are an estimated 14,000 to 19,000 Scimitar-horned Oryx in captivity around the world.

LIFESPAN: Unknown in the wild, but they can live up to 28 years in captivity.

RANGE: Formerly north and south of Sahara in sub-desert habitat from the Atlantic coast to the Nile. Reintroduced populations exist in Tunisia, Morocco and Senegal.

THREATS: Over-hunting, habitat destruction, competition with domestic livestock, drought and political instability.

 WHAT YOU CAN DO...

- Support the work of Marwell Wildlife (www.marwell.org.uk) by making a donation towards the Scimitar-horned Oryx conservation programme. The money raised will help Marwell Wildlife's conservation work with oryx in North Africa, and protect its habitat and other species that live there.

- Find out more about Marwell Wildlife's conservation work in North Africa by logging on to www.marwell.org.uk.

SEALS
(OF THE LAKES OF EASTERN EUROPE AND CENTRAL ASIA)

'ALL THE SPECIES AND SUBSPECIES OF RINGED SEAL IN THE EASTERN EUROPEAN LAKES HAVE SUFFERED POPULATION DECLINES OF MORE THAN 75% IN A CENTURY'
SEAL CONSERVATION SOCIETY

From the northern Baltic, stretching across Finland and Russia, there is a series of landlocked water bodies (Lakes Ladoga, Saimaa, Baikal and the Caspian Sea) inhabited by isolated seal populations related to the Arctic Ringed Seal. The original numbers of these seals was roughly proportional to the size of the lake, the largest being the Caspian, while the smallest was Saimaa. Except for Baikal Seals, where earlier and present population size is uncertain, all these seals have declined by more than 75% since 1900.

The main cause of the decline has been hunting. In recent years the accidental catching of pups in fishing gear is a particular threat to the Saimaa, Ladoga and Caspian Seals; the Baltic and possibly also Caspian Seals have suffered low fertility due to organochlorine pollutants; and there have been epidemics of canine distemper virus in Caspian and Baikal Seals.

All of these seals breed on the winter ice and therefore all of these populations are highly vulnerable to the effects of warmer winters. The breeding ice habitat may also be at risk from industrial icebreakers in the Baltic and Caspian, and activities including skidoos in Ladoga and Baikal.

All these landlocked seals are vulnerable to ecosystem degradation and reduction in fish stocks and also to coastal habitat loss due to human development and activity.

SCIENTIFIC NAMES: *Pusa hispida botnica* (Baltic Ringed Seal); *P.h. ladogensis* (Ladoga Ringed Seal); *P.h. saimensis* (Saimaa Ringed Seal); *P. caspica* (Caspian Seal – pictured right); *P. sibirica* (Baikal Seal)

SIZE: Varies. Baltic Ringed Seals are the largest of the subspecies measuring up to 1.75m.

STATUS: While IUCN status for some species is Least Concern, Baltic and Ladoga populations are considered to be Vulnerable and the Caspian and Saimaa Seals Endangered, the latter possibly the most endangered seal in the world.

SIZE: Adults about 1-1.5m.

POPULATION: 6,000 (Baltic); 5,000 (Ladoga); 310 (Saimaa); 100,000 (Caspian); unknown, but 80 to 100,000 suggested (Baikal).

LIFESPAN: Maximum longevity about 40-50 years.

RANGE: Only in the isolated lakes and seas.

THREATS: Hunting, fisheries bycatch, organochlorine pollution (lowered fertility), disease epidemics; industrial development, habitat loss.

SEAL
CONSERVATION SOCIETY

WHAT YOU CAN DO...

- Check the Seal Conservation Society's website, www.pinnipeds.org, for ongoing news and ways of lending support, and check the seal species pages at www.iucnredlist.org.

- Visit, too, www.helcom.fi, for the Baltic Ringed Seal, www.sll.fi for the Saimaa Ringed Seal, www.caspianseal.org for the Caspian seal and www.baikal.ru for the Baikal Seal.

SHARP-TAILED SNAKE

'RESIDENTIAL DEVELOPMENT IS THE GREATEST THREAT TO THIS TINY AND HARMLESS SNAKE'
ISLANDS TRUST FUND

The Sharp-tailed Snake likes to live on Canada's Vancouver Island and Gulf Islands. Unfortunately, so does everyone else, and residential development is the greatest threat to this tiny, harmless snake.

We need to discover more about this reptile's habitat requirements, to better understand the size and extent of its populations. Once existing snake population sites are known, conservationists will be able to develop community awareness and help landowners make wise land-use decisions.

Meanwhile, developers and property owners can protect the 30cm, pencil-thick snake by avoiding construction or use of vehicles, cars, pesticides, lawnmowers or weed-eaters in its habitat. Local people can keep pets under control, remove invasive plant species, restore native vegetation and consider creating natural habitat shelters for the snakes on their land. The presence of this species is indicative of over 100 threatened and endangered species in associated ecosystems.

COMMON NAME: Sharp-tailed Snake

SCIENTIFIC NAME: *Contia tenuis*

SIZE: Up to 45cm in length.

STATUS: Endangered in Canada (according to the Committee on the Status of Endangered Species in Canada).

POPULATION: Not known, but very rare in Canada.

LIFESPAN: Up to nine years in the wild.

RANGE: There are 14 known populations, all within 50km of Victoria, BC (British Columbia).

THREATS: Habitat loss and fragmentation due to urban and residential development, habitat alteration by weeds, predation by introduced species, and loss of tiny populations due to chance disturbances.

ISLANDS TRUST FUND   WHAT YOU CAN DO...

- Landowners can protect sunny, south-facing rocky slopes by leaving natural covers and hiding places, controlling invasive plants, avoiding pesticides and keeping cats indoors.

- The Islands Trust Fund (www.islandstrustfund.bc.ca) and the Habitat Acquisition Trust (www.hat.bc.ca) welcome donations to assist them in protecting this rare habitat.

SHORT-BEAKED COMMON DOLPHIN

'APPROPRIATELY MANAGED MARINE PROTECTED AREAS CAN CONTRIBUTE TO DOLPHIN CONSERVATION BY PRESERVING THEIR PREY AND HABITAT'
OCEANCARE

The Mediterranean population of Common Dolphin has declined dramatically in recent decades. While the species remains abundant worldwide, including in the westernmost portion of the Mediterranean, it has virtually vanished from several parts of the region where it used to be common – including in the Adriatic Sea, Ionian Sea, Balearic Sea and Ligurian Sea. The decline is thought to be primarily a consequence of prey depletion by commercial fisheries, incidental mortality in fishing gear (particularly drift gill nets), habitat degradation and chemical pollution.

Notwithstanding the large number of existing laws, regulations and agreements that have been in place for decades, enforcement and tangible actions to prevent further population decline have been surprisingly few. Recovery of Common Dolphins depends on public support to individuals and political parties seeking conservation action to address the multiple causes of decline.

Types of action that can provide benefits include area-, season- or fishery-specific reductions in fishing effort, changes to fishing gear or fishing practices to reduce incidental mortality, and curtailment of inputs of toxic pollutants. Appropriately managed Marine Protected Areas can contribute to dolphin conservation by preserving their prey and habitat, reducing the risks of mortality in fishing gear, providing refuge from sources of disturbance, raising awareness, stimulating research and facilitating exchange of information.

COMMON NAME: Short-beaked Common Dolphin

SCIENTIFIC NAME: *Delphinus delphis*

SIZE: Up to 2m in length.

STATUS: Endangered (Mediterranean Sea); Least Concern (globally).

POPULATION: Short-beaked Common Dolphins have been declining in the Mediterranean Sea over the past decades. The species is still abundant in the westernmost portion of the region (Alboran Sea), but numbers decline steeply towards the east and only a few hundred may survive in the eastern basin.

LIFESPAN: Up to approximately 30 years.

RANGE: Widely distributed in tropical to cool temperate waters of the Atlantic and Pacific Oceans, from nearshore to open ocean waters. Separate subpopulations exist in the Mediterranean and Black Seas.

THREATS: Prey decline caused by overfishing and habitat degradation, incidental mortality in fishing gear, and chemical pollution.

ocean care
www.oceancare.org

WHAT YOU CAN DO...

- Participate in Mediterranean expeditions (www.dolphinbiology.org/expeditions) aimed to study declining groups of Short-beaked Common Dolphins and support conservation action in the region.

- Get informed about the threats to marine mammals and how you can help by joining OceanCare (www.oceancare.org).

SIAMESE CROCODILE

'ONLY AROUND 250 ADULT SIAMESE CROCODILES REMAIN IN THE
WILD, CHIEFLY IN THE REMOTEST HIGHLANDS OF CAMBODIA'
CAMBODIAN CROCODILE CONSERVATION PROGRAMME

Over the past 100 years, hunting, collection for trade and habitat destruction have eradicated the Siamese Crocodile from 99% of its historical range throughout South-east Asia. Declared 'extinct in the wild' by the IUCN in 1992, the species was rediscovered in 2000 during a survey led by Dr Jenny Daltry from Fauna & Flora International.

Today, only around 250 adult Siamese Crocodiles remain in the wild, chiefly in the remotest highlands of Cambodia. While the crocodile is a much-maligned creature in the western world and often seen as a terrifying man-eater, in Cambodia it is regarded as a spiritual animal, to be revered and honoured.

The Cambodian Crocodile Conservation Programme (CCCP) has been surveying crocodile populations throughout Cambodia, working hard towards protecting and saving the species from vanishing for ever. During these surveys, they have identified three critically important breeding populations in the Cardamom Mountains of south-western Cambodia, which represent a significant percentage of the global population of wild Siamese Crocodiles (possibly up to 60%)

The CCCP is working with local communities to conserve the species and their globally important wetlands, using scientific research and activities that achieve measurable outputs. Through the support of this programme these communities have successfully protected crocodiles from poaching, habitat degradation and human conflict.

COMMON NAME: Siamese Crocodile

SCIENTIFIC NAME: *Crocodylus siamensis*

SIZE: Up to 3m in length.

STATUS: Critically Endangered.

POPULATION: The population is estimated to be only around 250 in the wild.

LIFESPAN: The average life span is unknown.

RANGE: Historically, Cambodia, Burma, Laos, Vietnam, Indonesia, Brunei, East Malaysia, Thailand. Currently, Cambodia, Laos and Kalimantan. Reintroduced to Vietnam.

THREATS: Poaching, collection for trade, habitat loss and degradation, and entanglement in fishing gear.

WHAT YOU CAN DO...

- Don't buy crocodile skin products without knowing their provenance.

- Speak up for crocs! There are no known records of Siamese crocodiles ever intentionally attacking a human being, so don't perpetuate the myth of them being man-eaters!

SIBERIAN CRANE

'CRANES ARE BELOVED ON FIVE CONTINENTS AND YET ARE
ONE OF THE MOST THREATENED FAMILIES OF BIRDS ON EARTH'
INTERNATIONAL CRANE FOUNDATION

Worldwide, the sight and sound of cranes stir the spirit. Cranes are symbols of harmony, fidelity, good fortune and long life throughout many cultures but, in spite of this, they are one of the most threatened families of birds on Earth. Crane populations are declining for a variety of reasons, including illegal trade, human disturbance, political instability, environmental contamination and power line collisions. The unmanaged loss and degradation of wetlands and grasslands is the single largest threat to these birds.

The Siberian Crane is one of those most endangered. The species is now found in only two populations: the eastern and western. A central population of Siberian Cranes once nested in western Siberia and wintered in India. The last documented sighting of Siberian Cranes in India during the winter months came in 2002. Although there are credible reports of small numbers of birds in western Siberia, the Volga Delta of southern Russia and Kazakhstan, all but a few existing birds belong to the eastern population.

COMMON NAME: Siberian Crane
SCIENTIFIC NAME:
Leucogeranus leucogeranus
SIZE: Approx 140cm in height.
STATUS: Critically Endangered.
POPULATION: Around 3,500 to 4,000.
LIFESPAN: The oldest documented crane was a Siberian crane named Wolf, who died at the age of 83. Wolf is in the *Guinness World Records* Book.
RANGE: The eastern population breeds in north-eastern Siberia and winters at Poyang Lake in the middle Yangtze River Basin of China. The traditional wintering site for the western population, along the south coast of the Caspian Sea in Iran, has only had a single bird in recent winters.
THREATS: Loss and degradation of habitats along migratory routes and in wintering areas (conversion of wetlands, dam construction and water diversions), development of resource industries in critical habitat, hunting, human disturbance, inadequate protected area management and declining water quality that affects its preferred foods.

WHAT YOU CAN DO...

• Become a Crane 'parent' by adopting a Crane through the International Crane Foundation (ICF) (www.savingcranes.org). Money raised helps ICF protect cranes and their ecosystems around the world.

• Learn about Siberian Crane Flyway Coordination established under the UNEP Convention on the Conservation of Migratory Species' Memorandum of Understanding Concerning Conservation Measures for the Siberian Crane at http://sibeflyway.org/ and www.cms.int/species/siberian_crane/sib_bkrd.htm.

SIBERIAN TIGER

'I BELIEVE IT IS INDIVIDUAL PEOPLE THAT WE HAVE TO CHANGE – ONE PERSON AT A TIME, ONE COMMUNITY AT A TIME, ONE COUNTRY AT A TIME – TO HAVE ANY LONG-TERM, SUSTAINED ENVIRONMENTAL IMPACT'
RARE

The Hunchun Nature Reserve in the snow-covered Jilin province is home to one-third of China's last remaining Siberian Tigers and sits at the border of China, Russia and North Korea. Rare Conservation Fellow Lang Jianmin, an employee of the nature reserve, realised that illegal wild game poaching was decreasing the prey population for Siberian Tigers, and posed a significant threat to tigers themselves. To protect the tiger, he knew he needed to do more than tell poachers to stop. To alter their actions, he would need first to change their hearts and minds.

Lang applied to Rare's unique programme designed to inspire change so both people and nature thrive. He launched a marketing campaign to help raise awareness and generate public support for the tiger. He reached out to local restaurants to stop serving wild game. He established farmer patrol teams to remove snares, and set up a system of subsidies, including the provision of bee boxes for restaurant owners who stopped serving tiger prey on their menus. He essentially created an atmosphere where selling and eating wild game became socially unacceptable. In two years, monthly incidents of poaching decreased from 23 to six and the percentage of villagers who eat wild game dropped from 56% to 18%.

'I hoped the people could be proud of the tiger,' said Lang, 'and now I am proud of them.'

COMMON NAME: Siberian Tiger
SCIENTIFIC NAME: *Panthera tigris altaica*
SIZE: 2.4 to 3.7m in length.
STATUS: Endangered.
POPULATION: 350-400.
LIFESPAN: 14 years in the wild.
RANGE: Boreal forest, China, North Korea and Russia.
THREATS: Habitat destruction and poaching of tigers and their prey.

WHAT YOU CAN DO...

- Find out more about innovative conservation efforts in tiger habitat in China and other areas around the world at www.rareconservation.org.

- As Henry David Thoreau said: 'Things do not change, we do.' You may live far from the tiger, but your actions impact the world we share with wildlife. Inspire change in your community.

- You can help stop habitat loss by buying products from sustainable forestry and agricultural operations.

SNOW LEOPARD

'TO SAVE THE SNOW LEOPARD WE NEED A FAR BETTER UNDERSTANDING OF ITS NEEDS, BEHAVIOUR AND HOW IT IS AFFECTED BY THE HUMANS AND LIVESTOCK WHICH SHARE ITS MOUNTAIN HOME'
DAVID SHEPHERD WILDLIFE FOUNDATION

Known throughout the world for its beautiful fur and elusive behaviour, the endangered Snow Leopard is found in the rugged mountains of central Asia. Snow Leopards are perfectly adapted to the cold, barren landscape of their high-altitude home, which ranges from 1,000 to 5,400m above sea level. Round, short ears reduce heat loss; wide, short nasal cavities heat the chilled air before it reaches their lungs; extra-large paws stop them sinking into the snow; and their long, thick tail aids balance and acts as a 'scarf' to keep them warm.

While the Snow Leopard is a top predator in its mountain ecosystem, human threats – including poaching, habitat degradation and retaliation killings – have created an uncertain future for this beautiful cat. Despite national and international laws to protect them, Snow Leopards are still being killed for their pelts, skin and bones, which are traded illegally. Unsustainable development and a boom in mining also threatens their habitat and many are killed by herders in retaliation following Snow Leopard attacks on their livestock.

The David Shepherd Wildlife Foundation funds work to find out more about these elusive cats and to support the people sharing their habitat. Projects include scientific research through the use of radio collaring, mapping where their territories overlap with human settlements and identifying possible conflict points; a livestock insurance programme to compensate herders for their losses; and a handicraft programme that engages herders in alternative income generation.

COMMON NAME: Snow Leopard

SCIENTIFIC NAME: *Uncia uncia*

SIZE: 75-130cm in length with a tail length of up to 100cm. Shoulder height about 60cm.

STATUS: Endangered.

POPULATION: Between 3,500 and 6,500. There is no exact figure because Snow Leopards are so elusive and inhabit such harsh and remote habitat that they are rarely seen.

LIFESPAN: Life is hard in the wild and lifespans are estimated to be between 10-13 years; up to 22 years in captivity.

RANGE: Snow Leopards live in fragmented populations throughout the mountains of central and south Asia.

THREATS: Illegal hunting for the fur trade, and trade in bones for traditional Asian medicine; loss of wild prey; retaliation killings by herders to protect their livestock; habitat loss; and lack of effective protection, awareness and support.

David Shepherd
Wildlife Foundation

WHAT YOU CAN DO...

- Find out more and donate to support Snow Leopard monitoring, scientific research, community education and awareness, and community enterprise schemes through the David Shepherd Wildlife Foundation at www.davidshepherd.org.

SOUTH CHINA TIGER

'DRIVEN FROM ITS HOME AND HUNTED TO NEAR EXTINCTION, FEWER THAN 100 OF THESE MAGNIFICENT ANIMALS ARE LEFT ALIVE TODAY'
SAVE CHINA'S TIGERS

The South China Tiger is the most endangered of the six remaining subspecies. In the 1950s, there were 4,000 tigers in China, but the effects of uncontrolled hunting, compounded by heavy deforestation and a likely reduction in the tiger's prey, meant that numbers fell very rapidly. There are now fewer than 100 left, and most of these are in zoos. Extinction in the wild is a very real possibility.

This a terrible fate for the subspecies acknowledged to be the ancestor of all modern tigers. It is the smallest tiger and an adaptable animal that enjoyed a prosperous existence until humans took over their last bit of land – the mountains.

The aim of Save China's Tigers is to raise awareness of the plight of the South China Tiger and to implement an innovative conservation model that includes a 300km² reserve in South Africa to breed and 're-wild' zoo-bred animals for the eventual reintroduction to vast protected reserves in China.

COMMON NAME: South China Tiger
SCIENTIFIC NAME: *Panthera tigris amoyensis*
SIZE: Males up to 2.6cm in length. Females up to 2.3cm.
STATUS: Critically Endangered.
POPULATION: Some estimate only a few South China Tigers remain in the wild while approximately 100 survive in captivity.
LIFESPAN: On average, tigers will live for 10-15 years out in the wild, and 16-20 years in captivity.
RANGE: In the wild, last known south of the Yangtze River, south China.
THREATS: Hunting and habitat destruction.

Save China's Tigers WHAT YOU CAN DO...

- Visit our website to learn more about the South China Tiger, see tiger pictures, make a donation, adopt a tiger or visit our eStore. For further information on Save China's Tigers, visit www.savechinastigers.org or contact: info@savechinastigers.org.

SPECTACLED BEAR

'BY CREATING MORE PROTECTED FORESTS THERE COULD STILL BE
A WAY TO HELP THIS IMPRESSIVE BEAR FROM FACING EXTINCTION'
RAINFOREST CONCERN

The Spectacled Bear, named for the white ring marks that some of them have around their eyes, is also known as the Andean Bear. It is among the smallest members of the bear family and the only species of bear found in South America. They are generally solitary animals and come together just for breeding.

The bears live in a wide range of habitats from 250m to 4,500m above sea level, but as shy creatures their preference is for undisturbed cloud forest, paramo and high grasslands. These bears are omnivores, feeding on berries, and plants such as bromeliads and palms, as well as insects, small rodents, birds and very occasionally cattle and dead carcasses they come across. They cover very large distances, of up to 60km^2, searching for food and can be found on platforms they have made up trees when there is fruit in season, which makes them extremely important seed dispersers for these important ecosystems they inhabit.

Fragmentation of their habitat due to farming, roads and mining have led to a decline in their population numbers and puts them at high risk when they are reduced to searching for food on farmers' land. By creating more protected forests and connecting fragmented areas as wildlife corridors, as well as teaching people about their importance, there could still be a way to help this impressive bear from facing extinction.

COMMON NAME: Spectacled Bear, Andean Bear

SCIENTIFIC NAME: *Tremarctos ornatus*

SIZE: 120-200cm in length. Shoulder height 60-90cm.

STATUS: Listed as Vulnerable (facing high risk of Extinction in the wild).

POPULATION: No complete study, varying estimates from 3,000 to 30,000 individuals, but declining due to fragmentation of habitat.

LIFESPAN: Spectacled Bears live up to an average of 20 years in the wild.

RANGE: Found in the Andes from western Venezuela through Colombia, Ecuador, Bolivia, possibly as far as north-west Argentina.

THREATS: Man-made habitat loss and fragmentation due to farming, roads and logging, killed to keep off crops or to sell parts for medicinal use.

WHAT YOU CAN DO...

• Sponsor an acre of forest (www.rainforestconcern.org) to save prime Spectacled Bear habitat in Ecuador and Colombia.

• You can offset your carbon emissions with Forest Credits; to read more about it, visit www.forestcredits.org.uk.

SPINY SEAHORSE

'THE COLLECTION OF SEAHORSES FROM THE WILD NEEDS TO BE BANNED'
THE SEAHORSE TRUST

Many people think of seahorses as being rather exotic fish, inhabiting hot tropical waters and swimming amongst the coral. It therefore often comes as a surprise to find there are not just one, but two, species of seahorse in the waters of the British Isles, Ireland and throughout Europe: the Short-snouted Seahorse (*Hippocampus hippocampus*) and the Spiny Seahorse (*Hippocampus guttulatus*).

The larger of the two is the Spiny Seahorse, which grows up to seven inches in length. It is a big seahorse with an impressive mane of appendages, designed for camouflage, on its head and neck, and down the upper part of the back, giving it its very descriptive name.

Seahorses are collected for a variety of reasons such as the traditional medicine, curio and pet trades, and they are also disappearing in some areas due to pollution, habitat loss and sedimentation, which smothers the habitat they live in, killing off everything that lives there.

Traditionally, Spiny Seahorses have been associated with seagrass beds, but research by The Seahorse Trust shows that they can occupy quite a wide range of algae-covered areas. These areas need to be protected and the collection of seahorses from the wild needs to be banned.

The
Seahorse
Trust

COMMON NAME: Spiny Seahorse

SCIENTIFIC NAME: *Hippocampus guttulatus*

SIZE: Up to 17cm in length.

STATUS: Highly Endangered and data deficient. They are fully protected under the Wildlife and Countryside Act 1981.

POPULATION: Not entirely known, but not considered to be common.

LIFESPAN: In captivity they have been known to live up to 12 years. In the wild the natural lifespan is estimated between eight and 10 years.

RANGE: All around Ireland, along the south coast of England, up the west coast around Wales and as far north as the Shetland Isles. In Europe, they are found off the coasts of France, Belgium, the Netherlands, Spain, Portugal and in the Bay of Biscay, and throughout the Mediterranean and Black Seas.

THREATS: Under major threat from overfishing for the traditional medicine, pet and curio trades. They are also under major threat through habitat loss, pollution and as a bycatch in the fishing industry.

WHAT YOU CAN DO...

- Don't buy any dried seahorses or starfish, shells or all of the marine creatures offered for sale by seaside shops. They are never sustainably caught as the shops state.

- Don't buy wild caught seahorses as pets as they will not survive without specialist care.

- Find out more about The Seahorse Trust and the work it does through the British Seahorse Survey. Visit our websites at www.theseahorsetrust.org and www.britishseahorsesurvey.org.

SPOON-BILLED SANDPIPER

'THE SPOON-BILLED SANDPIPER IS HURTLING TOWARDS EXTINCTION PERHAPS FASTER THAN ANY OTHER BIRD SPECIES'
WILDFOWL & WETLANDS TRUST

The Spoon-billed Sandpiper is hurtling towards extinction perhaps faster than any other bird species. Fewer than 100 pairs are thought to remain and the population is in free fall. Without urgent action, it could be gone within a decade.

A wading bird, barely larger than a sparrow, it is born with a spoon-shaped bill. No other bird hatches with such an adaptation.

Throughout its 8,000km migration from the coastal tundra of Russia's far east to the tropics of South Asia, the Spoon-billed Sandpiper faces a multitude of threats.

Chief among them are illegal hunting, which is killing the young birds before they are old enough to breed, and the reclamation of coastal mudflats, which they depend on to rest and refuel on their long migration.

To safeguard against the total extinction of the Spoon-billed Sandpiper, experts have managed to secure eggs from the few remaining nests in order to start a conservation breeding programme.

An urgent imperative is to tackle illegal hunting and the loss of wetlands. Conservationists working with villagers in Burma and Bangladesh have already started to ease the pressure of hunting on wading birds.

The hope is that the problems that the Spoon-billed Sandpiper faces can be solved. Then the conservation breeding programme will be producing eggs that can be hatched and released back into an environment that is far safer for this unique and charismatic bird.

COMMON NAME:
Spoon-billed Sandpiper

SCIENTIFIC NAME:
Eurynorhynchus pygmeus

SIZE: 140-160 cm in length.

STATUS: Critically Endangered.

POPULATION: In 2000 the global population was probably about 1,000 breeding pairs. Recently it has been falling by about a quarter each year. There are possibly fewer than 100 pairs left.

LIFESPAN: Their natural lifespan has not been studied, but it is likely to be about eight years. In their current decline the average lifespan is likely to be much lower than that.

RANGE: In June and July the birds breed on the coastal tundra of Chukotka in the Russian far east. They migrate along the east coast of Asia, stopping over to feed on tidal mudflats in the Yellow Sea. They spend the rest of the year in tropical South Asia. The Bay of Mottoma in Burma is the key non-breeding site.

THREATS: Loss of tidal mudflats to farming, industry and tourism along their migration route, eg Saemangeum in the Yellow Sea; and bycatch in the nets of shorebird hunters in South Asia.

 Wildfowl & Wetlands Trust WHAT YOU CAN DO...

- Donate to the Spoon-billed Sandpiper appeal at www.wwt.org.uk/sbs or join WWT (www.wwt.org.uk) to support wetlands and their wildlife.

SUMATRAN TIGER

'OVER THE PAST DECADE, THE WILD TIGER POPULATION HAS BEEN DECIMATED, WITH A MASSIVE 95% DROP IN NUMBERS. ONLY 300 WILD SUMATRAN TIGERS SURVIVE TODAY'
ZOOLOGICAL SOCIETY OF LONDON

As the last of the three Indonesian subspecies of tiger, Sumatran tigers are part of Indonesian cultural history, with their fierce beauty capturing the hearts of millions around the world. But their future is balanced on a knife edge. More than 30 Sumatran tigers were known to have been killed in 2012 alone and only around 300 remain in the wild.

The threats to these beautiful tigers are numerous and complex, and the Zoological Society of London (ZSL) is tackling them on many fronts. ZSL coordinates the global zoo conservation breeding programme for Sumatran tigers, which generates conservation support for wild tigers through the work of many zoos raising funds and awareness, and also provides valuable expertise and training. In the field, ZSL runs programmes on Sumatra, centred on the Berbak-Sembilang tiger landscape. Working in partnership with the Indonesian government, ZSL's Wildlife Crime and Conflict Response Teams remove snares, arrest intruders and support people affected by wildlife conflicts. Tigers that persist in taking livestock are relocated, and their movements tracked by ZSL field staff using satellite collars. Zoo expertise comes into this too; ZSL vets have provided practical veterinary training for their Indonesian counterparts.

Habitat protection is vital. ZSL works with industries such as palm oil to mitigate their impact on biodiversity, making production more sustainable. ZSL is also exploring innovative finance programmes that will make the Sumatran forests worth more to Indonesia's people standing up than chopped down, guaranteeing a safe home for tigers long into the future.

COMMON NAME: Sumatran Tiger
SCIENTIFIC NAME: *Panthera tigris sumatrae*
SIZE: Up to 2.3m in length.
STATUS: Critically Endangered.
POPULATION: About 300 wild individuals.
LIFESPAN: Probably less than 15 years in the wild, but up to around 20 in zoos.
RANGE: Distributed across remaining forested areas in Sumatra, both in protected areas and in other remaining forests.
THREATS: Killing of tigers for the illegal trade in their body parts and in retaliation to conflict incidents, killing of tiger prey species, habitat fragmentation and habitat loss.

WHAT YOU CAN DO...

- Visit Tiger Territory, the new flagship exhibit at ZSL London Zoo, to find out more about Sumatran Tigers.
- Join ZSL (www.zsl.org) and support its mission to conserve Sumatran Tigers and their habitats.

TASMANIAN WEDGE-TAILED EAGLE

'THIS EAGLE COULD BE ON THE BRINK OF EXTINCTION IN TASMANIA
IF DESTRUCTION OF THE STATE'S NATIVE FORESTS CONTINUES'
THE WILDERNESS SOCIETY AUSTRALIA

Big enough to hunt kangaroos, Tasmanian Wedge-tailed Eagles are a rare subspecies of Australia's largest bird of prey, the Wedge-tailed Eagle. Monarchs of the forest, they can soar more than 2km above the ground, and identify prey from over 1.5km away. Sensitive to disturbance, they nest in secluded trees, sometimes atop the loftiest ones in Tasmania's old-growth forests – the tallest hardwood forests on Earth.

But perhaps not for much longer. Farmers shoot them, and logging companies clearcut their forests and export the wood to Japan's paper-making factories.

It is estimated that there are now fewer than 1,500 Tasmanian Wedge-tailed Eagles left, including about 130 pairs successfully breeding each year. They are listed by the Australian government as endangered.

Breeding pairs, who mate for life, usually produce only one egg per year, and only half of these survive.

COMMON NAME: Tasmanian Wedge-tailed Eagle

SCIENTIFIC NAME: *Aquila audax fleayi*

SIZE: Up to 110cm in length with a wingspan of up to 2.3m.

STATUS: Endangered.

POPULATION: Fewer than 1,500 birds; about 130 successfully breeding pairs.

LIFESPAN: Over 20 years.

RANGE: Australian state of Tasmania.

THREATS: Logging, shooting and land-clearing. Collisions with powerlines, vehicles and wind turbines. Disturbance of nests – for example, by encroaching logging operations. Also, loggers poison native marsupials to stop them feeding on saplings, and the poison is passed on to the eagles which feed on their carcasses. The long-term impacts of this on the eagle are not yet known.

THE WILDERNESS SOCIETY

WHAT YOU CAN DO...

- Visit The Wilderness Society Australia's website to find out more about the campaign to protect Tasmania's old-growth forests and wildlife: www.wilderness.org.au.

- Please write to the Australian Prime Minister, Parliament House, Canberra ACT 2600, Australia, asking for support in protecting Tasmania's old-growth forests.

TOMISTOMA

'DESPITE THE WIDE CURRENT DISTRIBUTION, IT IS LIKELY THAT MOST REMNANT BREEDING POPULATIONS OF TOMISTOMA ARE THREATENED'
EUROPEAN ASSOCIATION OF ZOOS AND AQUARIA

Tomistoma (formerly called 'False Gavial or Gharial', reflecting its superficial similarity to the Gharial of India and neighbouring countries) is a freshwater, mound-nesting crocodilian with a distinctively long, narrow snout. It is one of the largest crocodilians, with males attaining lengths of up to 5m. The current distribution of Tomistoma extends over lowland regions of eastern Sumatra, Kalimantan and western Java (Indonesia), and Sarawak and Peninsular Malaysia where it occurs in lowland swamps, rivers, lakes and peatswamp forests.

Little data is available on Tomistoma biology and nesting ecology: fewer than 20 wild nests have been documented. Most nests were situated at the base of large trees, containing relatively small clutches of 13-35 eggs. Tomistoma feeds on a range of prey, including fish, birds, and mammals, such as monkeys.

Despite the wide current distribution, it is likely that most remnant breeding populations of Tomistoma are threatened. Severe loss of swamp forest has occurred in the past two decades at most documented Tomistoma localities in Sumatra and Kalimantan, due to forest fire, logging, plantation development and/or drainage. Although the species no longer appears to be subject to targeted hunting, eggs and young are collected opportunistically by local communities, and adults sometimes drown in fishing nets.

COMMON NAMES: Tomistoma, False Gharial, Malay Gharial

SCIENTIFIC NAME: *Tomistoma schlegelii*

STATUS: Listed in CITES, Appendix I and classified as Endangered on the IUCN Red List.

SIZE: Adults commonly grow to 3-4m, sometimes 5m.

POPULATION: An estimate of fewer than 2,500 mature adults was agreed by a consensus of active researchers as a cautious figure.

LIFESPAN: Average lifespan in the wild: 40-60 years.

RANGE: Widespread, although at a low density, throughout large areas of eastern Sumatra, western Java, Kalimantan and Sarawak, and still persists in Peninsular Malaysia.

THREATS: The principal threat to T. schlegelii is severe and continuing loss of swamp forest, mainly due to logging, fire, drainage, and plantation development. Other threats include entanglement in fishing gear, and low-level opportunistic removal of T. schlegelii from the wild.

WHAT YOU CAN DO...

- Habitats in South-east Asia are destroyed to provide space for huge oil palm plantations. Please try to avoid buying unsustainable and uncertified palm oil. To help you choose responsible alternatives, a white list of palm oil-free products is available from www.orangutans.com.au.

- Help save endangered species in South-east Asia by making a donation via www.southeastasiacampaign.org. The EAZA IUCN SSC Southeast Asia Campaign has selected six conservation projects, including the Tomistoma project, that focus on those species and habitats that need urgent support.

TRINIDAD PIPING-GUAN

'HUNTING AND HABITAT LOSS HAS DRIVEN GUAN NUMBERS DOWN:
THEY ARE NOW AT RISK OF EXTINCTION'
WORLD PHEASANT ASSOCIATION

Did you know that cracids are threatened? Do you even know what a cracid is? Should you be worried about them?

Cracids are a group of about 50 medium- to large-bodied bird species similar in appearance to turkeys. They include guans and curassows, and they come from the Neotropics, where they are often heavily hunted and therefore at risk of extinction in many places. The Trinidad Piping-guan is one of the most threatened species, although a misleading picture is given by habituated birds often seen by visiting birdwatchers. A combination of hunting and habitat loss has driven numbers down so that it is difficult to encounter the bird outside the one or two places where the species is regularly seen by birdwatching groups.

Recent conservation initiatives have seen the species designated as an Environmentally Sensitive Species and part of its geographic range an Environmentally Sensitive Area. Despite these advances, and the gathering of new information, it remains poorly known and in perilously low numbers.

COMMON NAME: Trinidad Piping-guan, or Pawi (local name)

SCIENTIFIC NAME: *Pipile pipile*

SIZE: 60cm in length.

STATUS: Critically Endangered.

POPULATION: Very difficult to determine reliably, but the species' range is only about 150km^2 in suitable habitat, where it is thought that there are fewer than 200 individuals remaining.

LIFESPAN: Not known.

RANGE: Known only from the Northern Range in north-eastern Trinidad, West Indies.

THREATS: Habitat loss and hunting across its limited range.

WHAT YOU CAN DO...

- Promote responsible birdwatching tourism in Trinidad so that local communities benefit from the interest and money that the pawi (as it is known locally) brings.

- Join the World Pheasant Association and support its work on critically endangered species by visiting www.pheasant.org.uk.

TRISTAN ALBATROSS

'BEING CAUGHT AS BYCATCH BY LONGLINE FISHING VESSELS IMPACTS MANY ALBATROSS SPECIES AND, AS A RESULT, 17 OF THE 22 ALBATROSS SPECIES ARE NOW THREATENED WITH EXTINCTION'
RSPB

The Critically Endangered Tristan Albatross is one of the largest flying birds on the planet, with a wingspan that can exceed 3m. It is also one of the most threatened: its population is declining at nearly 3% per year.

The decline is partly due to albatrosses being caught as bycatch by longline fishing vessels: birds dive on baited hooks, become caught and drown. This issue impacts many albatross species and, as a result, 17 of the 22 albatross species are now threatened with extinction.

The Tristan Albatross is not only threatened at sea, it also suffers at its only breeding site on Gough Island, in the UK Overseas Territory of Tristan da Cunha. Here, RSPB scientists discovered that introduced mice are killing the chicks by eating them alive.

In 2005, the RSPB set up the Albatross Task Force – a global team that braves the high seas, working directly with fishermen to reduce the number of birds caught. In South Africa, the number has already reduced by 80%. Similar work is being undertaken with other key fleets. The RSPB is also working with the Tristan da Cunha government to scope the feasibility of eradicating mice from Gough.

COMMON NAME: Tristan Albatross

SCIENTIFIC NAME: *Diomedea dabbenena*

SIZE: Up to 110cm in height with a wingspan of up to 3.5m.

STATUS: Critically Endangered.

POPULATION: Fewer than 11,000 individuals/1,700 breeding pairs per year, thought to be decreasing at nearly 3% per year.

LIFESPAN: At least 40-60 years.

RANGE: Across the southern Atlantic Ocean, predominantly between 30-45 degrees south.

THREATS: Longline fishing, mice predating chicks on the island.

WHAT YOU CAN DO...

- Join the RSPB from £3 a month by visiting www.rspb.org.uk or by calling 01767 693680.

- Help the Albatross Task Force by supporting the RSPB's Save the Albatross campaign. Visit www.rspb.org.uk/savethealbatross.

WOOLLY MONKEY

'SERIOUSLY THREATENED DUE TO DEFORESTATION,
HUNTING FOR BUSHMEAT AND THE PRIMATE PET TRADE'
WILD FUTURES

Woolly Monkeys are one of the largest of the South American primates.
They live in a wide range of sites in the tropical forests in the middle and
upper Amazon basin, with five species (recognised within two genera) found
over South America. They are arboreal and rarely venture to the forest
floor, spending most of their time up to 50m high in the canopy. Their most
striking adaptation is their fully prehensile tail, which acts as a powerful
fifth limb and enables them to forage while hanging from branches.

Woolly Monkeys live in social groups of up to 45 individuals and require
large areas of primary forest to sustain their numbers. Unfortunately, their
habitat is increasingly fragmented due to human activity and their survival
is also threatened by hunting for bushmeat. In addition to this, infant
woolly monkeys are still sold into the illegal pet trade by hunters.

Yellow-tailed Woolly Monkeys are now recognised as belonging to a
separate genus from the other woolly monkeys. Endemic to Peru, they are
Critically Endangered. Wild Futures, the charity that provides a home to
victims of the UK pet trade at The Monkey Sanctuary in Cornwall, supports
vital conservation and research projects so that these beautiful monkeys and
their natural habitat can be saved.

COMMON NAMES: Brown Woolly
Monkey, Grey Woolly Monkey,
Colombian Woolly Monkey, Silvery
Woolly Monkey and Yellow-tailed
Woolly Monkey

SCIENTIFIC NAMES: *Lagothrix
lagotricha, Lagothrix cana, Lagothrix
lugens, Lagothrix poeppigii* and
Oreonax flavicauda

SIZE: Body length up to 60cm.
Tail length up to 70cm.

STATUS: From Vulnerable to
Critically Endangered, depending
on the species.

POPULATION: Unknown in the wild.

LIFESPAN: Around 25 years.

RANGE: Woolly monkeys live in
isolated pockets of the Amazon
rainforest and Andes mountain
slopes in South America.

THREATS: Woolly monkeys are
adapted to primary rainforest, so
the main threat to their survival
is habitat loss or fragmentation
due to logging (for agriculture,
timber, mining and road
construction). Hunting for
bushmeat and the primate pet
trade also pose serious threats.

**Wild
Futures**

Protecting primates and habitats worldwide

WHAT YOU CAN DO...

- Adopt a monkey (visit www.adoptamonkey.org). The money raised will help Wild Futures to offer sanctuary to
monkeys in need and to protect primates and their habitats worldwide.

- Join Wild Futures' campaign to end the primate pet trade or, to help make a real change, become a
Wild Futures Ambassador and help to raise awareness and fundraise for the charity in your local community.
Visit www.wildfutures.org for details. Wild Futures: registered charity no. 1102532.

YELLOW-EYED PENGUIN

'THE BIRDS' EXISTENCE, PARTICULARLY ON MAINLAND NEW ZEALAND, IS FRAGILE'
YELLOW-EYED PENGUIN TRUST

Fast and sleek, proud and upright, yet also the Charlie Chaplin of the animal world, yellow-eyed Penguins are a New Zealand icon. But they are a threatened species, and their iconic status brings with it the need to protect this vulnerable penguin, and to sensibly manage opportunities to enjoy its unique character.

The birds' existence, particularly on mainland New Zealand, is fragile: having evolved in the absence of land-based mammalian predators they are vulnerable to predation. Nevertheless, they are an adaptable species, and after the almost complete loss of their forested nesting grounds they have adjusted well to modified habitats.

Penguin numbers in New Zealand's South Island have substantially increased from a low of 190 pairs in 1990 to an estimated 442 breeding pairs in 2011-12. We can do little about their food supply or natural marine predators, but we can keep them safe in a protected environment ashore.

COMMON NAME:
Yellow-eyed Penguin

LATIN NAME: *Megadyptes antipodes*

SIZE: 62-79 cm in length.

STATUS: Endangered.

POPULATION: An estimated 442 breeding pairs on mainland New Zealand (2012), 180 pairs on Stewart Island and adjacent islands (2012), 1,200 pairs on sub-Antarctic islands (estimated 1992).

LIFESPAN: At least 22 years.

RANGE: Found only along the eastern coastline of the South Island of New Zealand, and on Stewart Island and the sub-Antarctic islands of Auckland and Campbell.

THREATS: Introduced mammalian predators to mainland New Zealand, such as dogs, cats, ferrets, stoats and livestock disturbance. Natural predators are sea lions and large predatory fish.

WHAT YOU CAN DO...

- Find out more about the Yellow-eyed Penguin Trust by visiting www.yellow-eyedpenguin.org.nz.

- Become a member of, or make a donation to, the Yellow-eyed Penguin Trust and help save this unique penguin. You can do this online via the website, or send to PO Box 5409, Dunedin 9058, New Zealand.

CONSERVATION
GROUPS

CONSERVATION GROUPS

CONSERVATION GROUPS

PHOTO ACKNOWLEDGEMENTS

AFRICAN ELEPHANT: IFAW; AFRICAN PENGUIN: Eric Gevaert/Shutterstock; AMAZONIAN MANATEE: SeaPics.com; AMUR LEOPARD: Chris Humphries/Shutterstock; ANCIENT WOODLAND: The Woodland Trust; ANDEAN CONDOR: Iakov Filimonov/ Shutterstock; ARGALI SHEEP: David Kenny; ASIAN ELEPHANT: Mogens Trolle/Shutterstock; ASH: FLPA/Nicholas and Sherry Lu Aldridge; ASIAN ELEPHANT: Mogens Trolle/Shutterstock; AZRAQ KILLIFISH: Koji Kawai/Royal Society for the Conservation of Nature; BARBARY MACAQUE: Botond Horvath/Shutterstock; BASKING SHARK: Andrew Pearson; BECHSTEIN'S BAT: Hugh Clark/Bat Conservation Trust; BLACK POPLAR: Nick Spurling/FLPA; BLACK RHINOCEROS: Save the Rhino International; BLUE-GREY TAILDROPPER: Habitat Acquisition Trust; BLUE-THROATED MACAW: World Parrot Trust; BOTTLENOSE DOLPHIN: Willyam Bradberry/Shutterstock; BROWN HYENA: EcoPrint/Shutterstock; CHEETAH: Jason Prince/Shutterstock; CHIMPANZEE: Konrad Wothe/Minden Pictures/FLPA; COMMON CRANE: Tim Nevard/Pensthorpe Conservation Trust; COMMON DORMOUSE: Ian Pratt; COMMON HIPPOPOTAMUS: Anton Ivanov/Shutterstock; CORAL REEFS: Biosphere Expeditions; CORNCOCKLE: MarkMirror/Shutterstock; DALL'S PORPOISE: Hiroya Minakuchi/ Minden Pictures/FLPA RM; DELHI SANDS FLOWER-LOVING FLY: Guy Bruyea; DISTINGUISHED JUMPING SPIDER: PR Harvey; DRILL: Cyril Ruoso/Minden Pictures/FLPA RM; EASTERN LOWLAND GORILLA: Frans Lanting/FLPA; ETHIOPIAN WOLF: Burriard-Lucas; EURASIAN CURLEW: Paul Hillion; EURASIAN LYNX: KOO/Shutterstock; EUROPEAN STAG BEETLE: Florian Andronache/Shutterstock; FLORIDA PANTHER: US Fish and Wildlife Service; FOSA: Costas Anton Dumitrescu /Shutterstock; FRESHWATER PEARL MUSSEL: Freshwater Biological Association; GOULDIAN FINCH: Steve Murphy; GRANDIDIER'S BAOBAB: Arto Hakola/Shutterstock; GREAT CRESTED NEWT: Dave Kilby; GREATER BAMBOO LEMUR: Tony King/The Aspinall Foundation; GREEK RED DAMSELFLY: JP Boudot; GREEN TURTLE: SecondShot / Shutterstock; GREY NURSE SHARK: Ron & Valerie Taylor/Ardea; GURNEY'S PITTA: Boonchuay Promjiam/ Shutterstock; HAIRY-NOSED OTTER: Associated Press; HAWAIIAN COTTON TREE: Lyon Arboretum; HUMPHEAD WRASSE: Song Heming/Shutterstock; IRISH HARE: Mike Brown; JAVAN LEAF MONKEY: